Home Improvements

52 Easy Weekend Projects

Home Improvements

52 Easy Weekend Projects
Dan Ramsey

TAB BOOKS Inc.
Blue Ridge Summit, PA

This book is dedicated to Florence Delrow from the Carnation Boy.

FIRST EDITION
FIRST PRINTING

Copyright © 1989 by TAB BOOKS Inc.
Printed in the United States of America

Library of Congress Cataloging in Publication Data

Ramsey, Dan, 1945—
    Home improvements : 52 easy weekend projects / by Dan Ramsey.
        p. cm.
    Includes index.
    ISBN 0-8306-1448-6   ISBN 0-8306-3148-8 (pbk.)
    1. Dwellings—Remodeling.   2. Dwellings—Maintenance and repair.
  I. Title.
TH4826.R35   1989
643′.7—dc19   89-4271
                                                                  CIP

TAB BOOKS Inc. offers software for sale. For information and a catalog, please contact TAB Software Department, Blue Ridge Summit, PA 17294-0850.

Questions regarding the content of this book should be addressed to:

    Reader Inquiry Branch
    TAB BOOKS Inc.
    Blue Ridge Summit, PA 17294-0214

Edited by Cherie R. Blazer

Contents

Introduction

Americans spend over $100 billion a year on home improvements: remodeling, repairing, adding on, and sprucing up. Most consider the dollars they spend an investment in the value and the liveability of their home. And they're right. In fact, most home improvements do pay the homeowners back at least their cost on resale; some actually earn more. Here are the facts:

☐ A new second or third bathroom pays back 75 to 80 percent of its cost at resale.

☐ Room additions pay back from 80 to 100 percent of their cost when the home is sold.

☐ Wooden decks return 60 to 80 percent of the investment.

☐ Attic conversions increase the value of the home by 80 to 100 percent of the cost.

☐ Fireplaces earn homeowners a return of 80 to 95 percent of their cost.

☐ Closets and built-in storage pay homeowners back 90 to 100 percent of their original costs.

☐ Painting the exterior of your home will earn a 100 percent return of costs when you sell.

☐ Interior decorating pays back 80 to 100 percent of the costs on resale.

Remember: these returns are for contracted services. By doing the work yourself, you can reduce labor costs and actually earn a profit on carefully selected home improvements.

More importantly, you will increase your home's liveability by making fundamental improvements to it. A new bathroom, an attic study, a recreation room, a bay window, bookshelves, a new sink, a ceiling fan, a workshop—all will add to the day-to-day enjoyment of your home.

Home Improvements: 52 Easy Weekend Projects is specifically written to show you how to make such home improvements with smaller, easy-to-complete projects that can be tackled over a weekend. In fact, some projects can be completed in just a few hours. Others will require an evening or two during the week for preparation in order to complete them over a weekend. You'll probably find most of them to be quite enjoyable.

The book is developed in four sections, one for each season of the year. Each section offers 13 weekend projects that are most appropriate to that season. Of course, you can do most of them at any time of the week or the year.

Each project article is written so that it can easily be read in an evening during the week. You can then make a simple list of the items or materials you will need so that you work efficiently when you begin your project. Most projects are illustrated to help you better understand the project. Additional reading material, other TAB books by the author, are referred to for further information.

Whether you take on a few, a dozen, or all 52 projects, you'll find this book both informative and entertaining.

Acknowledgments

I gratefully acknowledge the assistance of the following resources in developing this book: Armstrong World Industries; Color Tile Supermart; California Redwood Association; Style-Tex; Hyde Manufacturing Co.; General Electric; NuTone; Tile Council of America; National Oak Flooring Manufacturers Association; Harris-Tarkett; Georgia-Pacific Corp.; Teco Inc.; Aromatic Red Cedar Closet Lining Manufacturers Association; Genova Inc.; Koppers Company; Sylvania; Loran Inc.; Builders Fence Co. Inc.; International Fence Industry Association; Sears, Roebuck & Co.; and Judy Ramsey.

Winter Projects

1

Refinish a Piece of Furniture

Refinishing wood furniture is a perfect weekend project. It requires little skill, few tools and materials, and short periods of work are sandwiched between long periods of inactivity (euphemistically called "drying time"). It can be done while sitting out on the back porch, or with newspapers strewn on the floor in front of the TV. Most of all, it offers a sense of accomplishment that is renewed every time you view your project.

The tools you'll need depend upon the project itself. Safety equipment such as goggles, rubber gloves, a work apron, and possibly a face mask, are vital. Stripping requires sandpaper and block, steel wool, a putty knife, and related tools. Finishing is done with brushes or a spray gun. Make sure you have enough drop cloths or newspaper on hand, so you don't damage a surface you hadn't intended to refinish.

REMOVING THE OLD FINISH

You will either want to strip the wood yourself, or hire a furniture stripping firm to do the job; it depends on the project. Keep in mind that to have it stripped, you must transport the piece to the stripping service; they will not come to you. This often rules out larger pieces such as pianos and cabinets, unless you have the money or equipment to move the furniture. If you use a stripping service, examine some samples of their work and get a written estimate of the cost before proceeding.

There are three ways you can strip off old varnish, shellac, or enamel: with abrasives, with chemicals, or with heat. Abrasives include sandpaper, steel wool, and rasps. A *rasp* is a rough scraper that can easily damage wood, so be careful.

Sandpaper and steel wool are selected according to their coarseness. Use the most coarse grade to remove initial loose finish, then progress to finer grades that feather the edges of remaining finishes or, if desired, smooth the bare wood that remains.

There are a variety of stripping chemicals available. All of these work by softening the chemicals within the old finish so that it can be removed with a scraper. Make sure that the stripper you purchase is designed for removing the specific finish. Not all strippers work equally well on paints, varnishes, urethanes, and other finishes. If in doubt, take a sample of the finish to your paint shop for a recommendation.

Heat removal is a newer concept for the do-it-yourselfer. It has become quickly popular because it can easily lift old finishes from wood surfaces in a matter of minutes with carefully applied heat and a scraper. Test the method on a back or underside of the piece of furniture before tackling the entire job. Don't use any heat source except one designed for heat stripping. Make sure that, if you are also using a chemical, the stripper is not flammable.

SELECTING FINISHES

There are many finishes available for refinishing wood furniture. Stains can be used to add color to the wood and enhance the grain, then a varnish, sealer, or wax overcoat applied. Varnishes withstand wear and hard scrubbing, and give wood the appearance of depth. Clear sealers are heat- and moisture-resistant, and darken wood to enhance grains and textures. Clear lacquer is an excellent finish for wood that will not come in contact with moisture. Wax finishes add a rich, soft luster to wood while providing some water resistance. Paint offers both color and protection. Talk to your paint retailer for specific recommendations, making sure to tell him for what purpose your project will be used.

APPLYING FINISH

Brushes are the most common tools for applying finish. For painting most wood furniture, a flat brush 2 to 2½ inches wide, with bristles 3 to 3¼ inches long is best. A flat or oval sash brush, 1½ inches wide with 2-inch bristles is recommended for trim and fine finishing. A 3½-inch brush is generally used for applying oil paints to large surfaces.

Spray cans offer the do-it-yourselfer the advantages of spray finishing without the cost and cleanup of large spray units. When spraying on finish, move side to side at an equal distance from the surface, beginning the stroke before reaching the wood surface and ending it after. This provides full and even coverage.

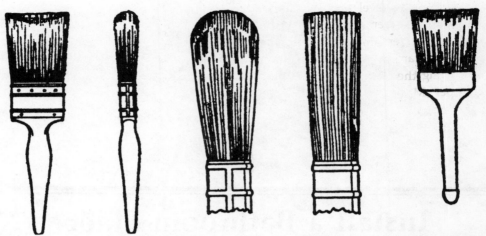

Fig. 1-1. Paintbrushes look alike. The three brushes on the right are flat wall brushes, which are contoured to paint smoothly and evenly. The left two are inferior brushes.

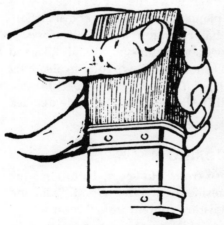

Fig. 1-2. Test the paintbrush for shape.

Fig. 1-3. The top illustration shows veneer pulling loose at the edge; the bottom shows veneer blisters.

It's best to begin your project on a hidden surface, such as the bottom of a chair seat or the back of a cabinet, so that you can determine how the wood will react to the finish and your application method. If such surfaces are not available, find a scrap of wood similar to your piece. As a last resort, test the finish on the piece, applying the finish lightly, in case it must be covered or removed.

2

Install a Bathroom Floor

One of the easiest and least expensive ways to improve the appearance of your bathroom is to install a new floor. An hour of planning, a few hours of installation, and $100 to $200 can transform a common bathroom into a decorative one.

And you can do it yourself. Laying a new floor requires no special skills and only a few inexpensive tools. This project will show you how. You can also refer to *Tile Floors* by Dan Ramsey (TAB Book 1998) or *The Complete Book of Bathrooms* by Judy and Dan Ramsey and Charles R. Self (TAB Book 2708) for more detailed instructions.

SELECTING FLOORING

There are many flooring materials to choose from. However, bathrooms are typically floored either with ceramic tile or resilient vinyl tile. Wood floors and carpeting are not appropriate due to the moisture content in bathrooms.

Ceramic tile is an excellent choice because of its durability and water resistance. Showers, especially, cause moisture to collect on walls and floors. Unglazed ceramic tile is preferable to glazed because it is more slip-resistant.

Resilient vinyl tile is usually less expensive and easier to install than ceramic tile, and comes in a variety of designs, patterns, and colors to match most decors.

The best place to start shopping for your bathroom flooring is a large building material store or flooring retailer that has displays to help you visualize your project. Take with you a scale drawing of your bathroom, which includes complete measurements and the locations of cabinets, lavatories, and other components attached to the floor. Also take some color samples of the interior you wish to match. Keep in mind as you browse that flooring patterns will look smaller in

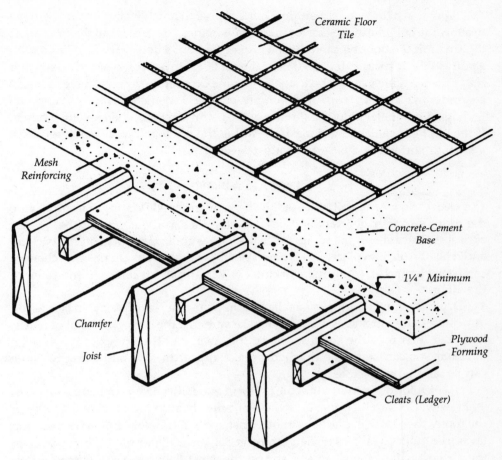

Fig. 2-1. Components of a ceramic tile floor.

the store than they will on your floor. A 6-inch square tile will be too large for a small bathroom floor.

PREPARING THE FLOOR

If your original floor lifts off easily, as carpeting or wood usually does, little preparation is necessary. Simply remove nails and make sure that the floor is smooth. However, if you are replacing linoleum, vinyl, or ceramic tile, you will have to either remove or cover the remaining adhesive in order to provide a perfectly smooth, clean surface for your new floor.

To remove existing sheet flooring, first cut the wear layer into narrow strips, then peel it off from the backing. Examine the remaining felt to determine how to best remove it. You might be able to scrape it off if you first apply dishwashing detergent and allow it to penetrate. Don't apply too much water or you will have to allow the subflooring to dry for many days before you can install the new floor.

Ceramic tile flooring can often be broken away at a doorway, then lifted with a putty knife or spatula. If the old floor cannot be removed easily or the underlying *mastic*, as the adhesive is called, does not come up evenly, you will have to install an underlayment. This involves simply cutting a ⅛-inch sheet of Philippine mahogany or similar plywood the size of the bathroom floor, then nailing it down. If the old floor remains, use mastic to install the plywood. Make sure you have a smooth surface as a base for your new floor.

INSTALLATION

The easiest floor to install is self-adhering resilient vinyl flooring. Simply divide the room into four quarters and begin laying tiles at the corner of the quarter closest to the center of the room. Once position is confirmed, peel off the backing and relay the tile into place. Lay it down slowly so that any slight position changes can easily be made. Continue working outward from the center of the room to the edges.

Dry-back vinyl flooring is installed in the same way, except that mastic is laid down just before the tile is placed. To make sure that the correct amount of mastic is spread, first read the suggestions on the label, and then practice. Laying too much mastic can make the finished project appear messy, but laying too little can be simply ineffective.

Sheet flooring is more difficult to lay in a small space, as a bathroom often is. However, it can be done. To install, cut the sheet to the outside diameter of the room, then lay it in place—without mastic—then trim for cabinets, pipes, and lavatories. Once you're satisfied that it is cut correctly, spread the mastic over the farthest half of the room and spread the sheet flooring. Then spread mastic on the half closest to the door and lay the remainder of the floor. By following this procedure, you won't walk in mastic or get trapped in a corner.

Installing ceramic tile is more difficult, but it also gives a richer appearance and is longer-lasting. Ceramic tiles come either loose or in 1-foot-square sheets on a net backing. Install them in the same manner as noted earlier: section the room into quarters and begin at the center. Use a grooved trowel to spread the mastic to the thickness recommended by the manufacturer. Lay the ceramic tile or sheet in place and make minor adjustments as needed. Make sure that tiles are aligned. Borrow or rent a tile cutter from the retailer to trim tile for walls and around objects.

Once the ceramic floor is finished, spread grout between the tiles. Mix powdered grout with water to the consistency of clay, then spread across the surface of the tile with a soft-surfaced grout trowel that forces it between the tile. Wash off the surface later with a wet cloth or rub it with dry grout to fill holes

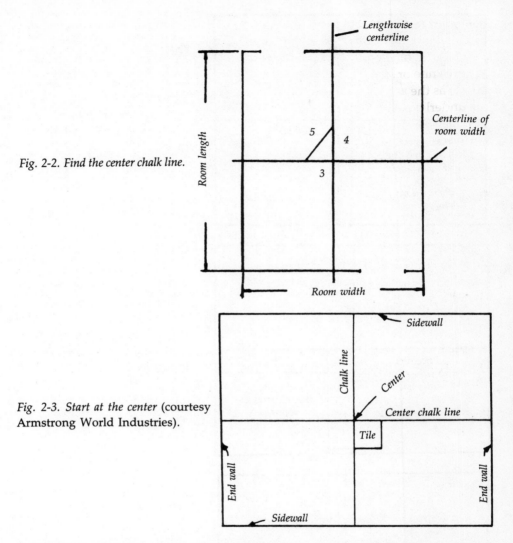

Fig. 2-2. *Find the center chalk line.*

Fig. 2-3. *Start at the center* (courtesy Armstrong World Industries).

and clean the tile. Once fully dry, special finishes can be installed to protect the grout from moisture and stains.

MAINTENANCE

The best bathroom floor maintenance is preventive. Make sure that spills, especially cosmetics, are quickly cleaned up. Check for condensation that collects on floors near baths, showers, lavatory tanks, and pipes. Periodically scrub the floor with a recommended cleaner. Vinyl tile is easier to maintain than the grout around ceramic tile, but there are grout cleaners that work well on floors as well as walls.

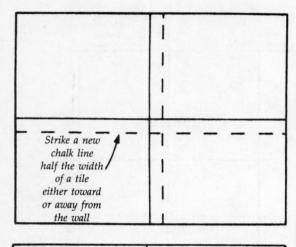

Strike a new
chalk line
half the width
of a tile
either toward
or away from
the wall

Fig. 2-4. Adjusted chalk line for beginning the installation (courtesy Armstrong World Industries).

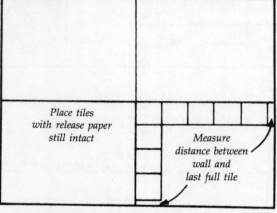

Place tiles
with release paper
still intact

Measure
distance between
wall and
last full tile

Fig. 2-5. Laying self-adhering floor tiles (courtesy Armstrong World Industries).

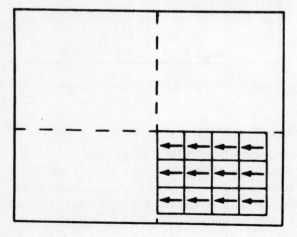

Fig. 2-6. Install tile with arrows on back pointing in the same direction (courtesy Armstrong World Industries).

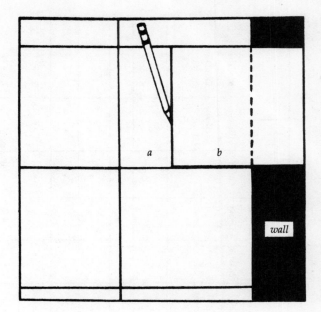

Fig. 2-7. Fitting a tile next to the wall (courtesy Armstrong World Industries).

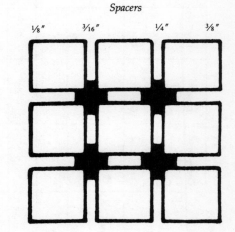

Fig. 2-8. Installing spacers between ceramic tiles (courtesy Color Tile Supermart).

Table 2-1. Grout Guide. (courtesy Tile Council of America)

Printed through the courtesy of the Materials & Methods Standards Association

A rubber faced trowel should be used when grouting glazed tile with sanded grout.

GROUT TYPE

	Commercial Portland Cement — Wall Use	Commercial Portland Cement — Floor Use	Sand-Portland Cement — Wall-Floor Use	Dry-Set Portland Cement — Wall-Floor Use	Latex Portland Cement (3)	Mastic (3)	Epoxy (1)(6)	Furan (1)(6)	Silicone or Urethane (2)	Modified Epoxy Emulsion (3)(6)
TILE TYPE										
GLAZED WALL TILE (More than 7% absorption)	•			•	•	•			•	
CERAMIC MOSAICS	•	•	•	•			•		•	•
QUARRY, PAVER & PACKING HOUSE TILE	•	•	•	•			•	•	•	•
AREAS OF USE										
Dry and intermittently wet areas	•	•	•	•	•	•	•	•	•	•
Areas subject to prolonged wetting	•	•	•	•			•	•	•	•
Exteriors	•	•	•	•	•(4)	•	•(4)	•(4)		•(4)
PERFORMANCE										
Stain Resistance (5)	D	C	E	D	B	A	A	A	A	B
Crack Resistance (5)	D	D	E	D	C	C	C	B	A Flexible	C
Colorability (5)	B	B	C	B	B	A	B	Black Only	Restricted	B

(1) Mainly used for chemical resistant properties.

(2) Special tools needed for proper application. Silicone, urethane and modified polyvinylchloride used in pregrouted ceramic tile sheets. Silicone grout should not be used on kitchen countertops or other food preparation surfaces unless it meets the requirements of FDA Regulation No. 21, CFE 177.2600.

(3) Special cleaning procedures and materials recommended.

(4) Follow manufacturer's directions.

(5) Five performance ratings—Best to Minimal (A B C D E).

(6) Epoxies are recommended for prolonged temperatures up to 140F, high temperature resistant epoxies and furans up to 350F.

3

Make More Storage Room

It seems that winter is the season that most clearly illustrates your lack of storage. Christmas lights and ornaments are searched out, winter clothing must be gathered together and hung in the back closet, winter tools are brought out of storage. Then, once the Christmas tree is down, it—and all those broken toys—must be placed in storage.

Of course, storage space is actually a year-round problem. Careful planning is necessary to ensure adequate storage space for family needs. Fortunately, with a small amount of money, and a weekend or two of your time, you can easily transform wasted space into storage. Included here are plans for additional closet, kitchen, and basement storage space, which can easily be modified for extra storage in a bathroom, attic, or garage.

CLOSETS

All clothes closets are basically the same. No matter what their shapes are, one of the following plans can be adapted. Dimensions may be increased or decreased, and the arrangement varied by adding hooks, trays, shelves, drawers, and racks. For clarity, the spacing of hung clothes is shown by lines drawn at right angles to the rods.

KITCHEN

One of the objectives of kitchen planning is to make the kitchen a more efficient work center. To accomplish this, modern kitchens are divided into work areas. An important part of design is sufficient storage space. As you plan, consider

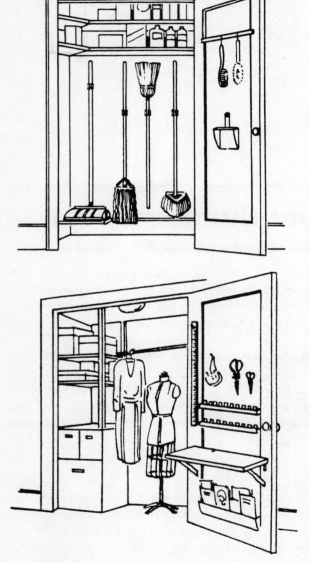

Fig. 3-1. Typical closet.

Fig. 3-2. A closet can become a sewing center.

the type of articles stored, space economy, flexibility, appearance, ease of cleaning, and cost. List the items to be stored, grouping them according to usage. Estimate the unit dimensions for each group of articles, allowing enough space for taking out and replacing. After estimating total space requirements for each group, plan details for each section of the storage space.

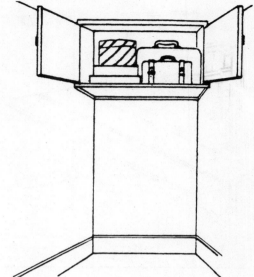

Fig. 3-3. Unused high spaces in closet can become storage.

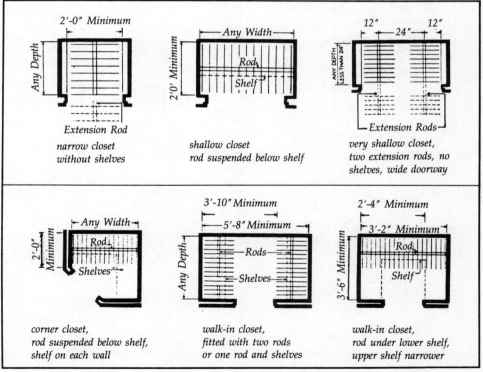

narrow closet
without shelves

shallow closet
rod suspended below shelf

very shallow closet,
two extension rods, no
shelves, wide doorway

corner closet,
rod suspended below shelf,
shelf on each wall

walk-in closet,
fitted with two rods
or one rod and shelves

walk-in closet,
rod under lower shelf,
upper shelf narrower

Fig. 3-4. Closet designs.

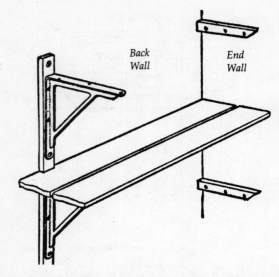

*Back
Wall*

*End
Wall*

Fig. 3-5. *Steel braces and wood
strips can support storage shelves.*

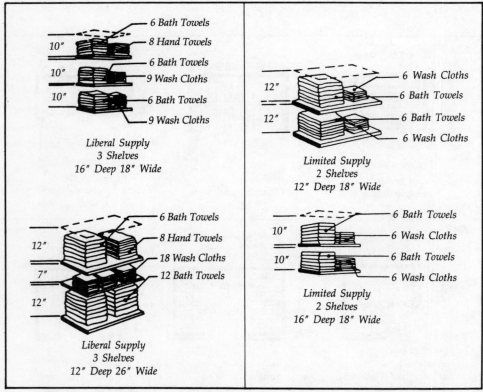

6 Bath Towels
8 Hand Towels
10"
6 Bath Towels
10"
9 Wash Cloths
10"
6 Bath Towels
9 Wash Cloths

*Liberal Supply
3 Shelves
16" Deep 18" Wide*

12"
6 Wash Cloths
6 Bath Towels
12"
6 Bath Towels
6 Wash Cloths

*Limited Supply
2 Shelves
12" Deep 18" Wide*

12"
6 Bath Towels
8 Hand Towels
18 Wash Cloths
7"
12 Bath Towels
12"

*Liberal Supply
3 Shelves
12" Deep 26" Wide*

6 Bath Towels
10"
6 Wash Cloths
6 Bath Towels
10"
6 Wash Cloths

*Limited Supply
2 Shelves
16" Deep 18" Wide*

Fig. 3-6. *Planning storage can make a linen closet more efficient.*

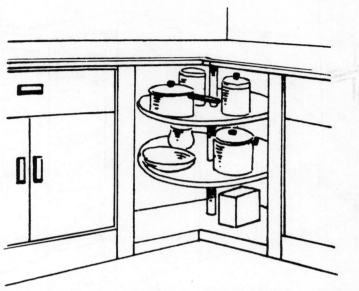

Fig. 3-7. A lazy Susan in the corner of a kitchen cabinet makes an otherwise unused space useable.

BASEMENT CLOSET

Although understair space in the upper floors of a house is usually devoted to closets, for some reason the space beneath basement stairs is often neglected. This is an excellent place to build a roomy storage closet. Even if the basement is not of the best quality, the closet can be used to store miscellaneous articles that take up too much valuable space in other closets, or that collect in odd corners about the house: outgrown children's play equipment, overalls and work clothing, or tools.

The size of your understairs basement storage closet, of course, depends upon available space. Measure the height and depth of the space, then purchase the materials you will need: a hollow-core prehung door, door latch kit, 2-×-4 studs, wallboard or paneling, shelving. Make sure the door will fit in the space provided. If not, you might want to construct a simple door using a 1-×-2-inch frame overlayed with paneling. Then construct a 2-×-sill and frame, spacing studs 24 inches apart. Install the door frame and door. Cover the studs with paneling or wallboard.

If your understairs space is deep, you might want to include a second, smaller door at the side of the closet to utilize the space at the back. Otherwise, the deep space can be used for storing ski equipment, sleds, or building materials.

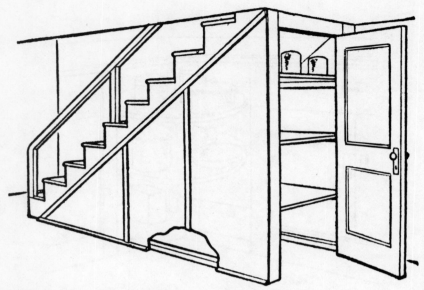

Fig. 3-8. *Large storage space is available under basement stairs.*

4

Organize Your Shop

Home improvements and repairs can be either drudgery or a rewarding hobby. The difference usually lies in having the proper tools and adequate workspace. Poor tools and workspace typically lead to poor workmanship—and frustration. Plan to devote at least one weekend to organizing your shop so that the tasks of the other weekends will be easier and more enjoyable.

An adequate shop doesn't have to be elaborate or expensive. A perfectly satisfactory job can be done with a few well-chosen tools, well arranged within limited space. In fact, many good shops have been built in cabinets, closets, or other small spaces. Planning is the key. Of course, there is no such thing as the "ideal" home workshop; some will have extensive electrical tools and materials, while others specialize in woodworking, or plumbing, or painting. The majority will combine some tools and materials for each of these do-it-yourself areas. Most importantly, your shop should be organized to keep everything in its logical place.

LOCATING THE WORKSHOP

Workshop space requirements can range from a shelf or a table to an entire room or group of rooms. Remember, though, that the smaller the space, the fewer improvements and repairs can be done. When selecting the appropriate location and space for your workshop, consider the following:

☐ Your workshop should have enough area to handle the kind of materials you will be using. Work requiring large lengths of lumber can only be done in a fairly large workshop, or in an area to which tools can easily be moved.

☐ Materials must easily be moved in and out with ease. The space should also have ample storage for basic materials. This is as simple as a few closet shelves for paints and painting supplies, to a garage where large sheets of paneling are stored and ripped.

☐ Your workshop should be convenient to the area where most improvements and repairs will be made. For example, a workshop for remodeling a bathroom and kitchen shouldn't be located in a distant garage. If possible, install it where tools are readily accessible as the job continues.

☐ The space should be reasonably dry and free of excessive dust. It should also be well ventilated, especially if you plan to use flammables or caustic chemicals.

☐ The best workshops have a natural source of light. However, all should have adequate light fixtures and ample electrical outlets to increase efficiency and safety.

☐ Your workshop should be located so that it doesn't become a safety hazard. Lock combustible materials in fireproof storage space. Don't allow waste materials to accumulate. An emergency exit should be readily available. Install a fire alarm and fire extinguisher.

☐ Plan your workshop for expansion. That is, consider where you would expand or move your shop if the need for more space arises.

The basement is the most common, and often most desirable, location for a workshop. It usually provides sufficient work and storage space for practically all types of home improvement projects. The major drawback to many basements is that they are damp, and moisture can rust tools and spoil materials. Before considering a basement for your workshop, be sure you will be able to make it dampproof, if it is not already.

The attic can often be used as a workshop. Depending on how your home is constructed, it is usually less desirable because of the difficulty of getting materials in and out. Attic work noises can reverberate throughout the house. Also, attics are typically hot in the summer and cold in the winter.

The garage is often a good location for a workshop, particularly a two-car or oversized garage. Of course, you will have to provide adequate heating and lighting to make your garage into a fully functional workshop.

Other areas of your home will work also. Your workshop can be combined with the addition of an extra bedroom, a family room, or a playroom, to make life more efficient and more fun.

EQUIPPING YOUR WORKSHOP

Once you've selected and measured your workspace, consider how you are going to equip it. Do your improvements require a large table or radial arm saw? Can you do much of your cutting with a portable power saw? Do you need long-term storage for finished wood? Will you need many nails, screws, and other fasteners, or just the basics? The best planning method is to lay out your tools on a garage or other floor as you would in your shop, grouping them together by function. Then mentally add the tools that you expect to acquire in the next few years. Move the tools around, considering how frequently they will be used. Place the most necessary tools on pegboards, and infrequently used tools in drawers, on shelves, or in boxes stored under your workbench.

Make sure that when you are equipping your workshop that you install ample electrical outlets for the power tools you require. The principle of a workshop is to be as efficient as possible; this means you can't spend half your time exchanging tools in a wall plug.

WORKBENCHES AND SHELVES

Finally, you're ready to install the furniture and fixtures that will help you work more efficiently. The primary workstation is typically a workbench. Its size

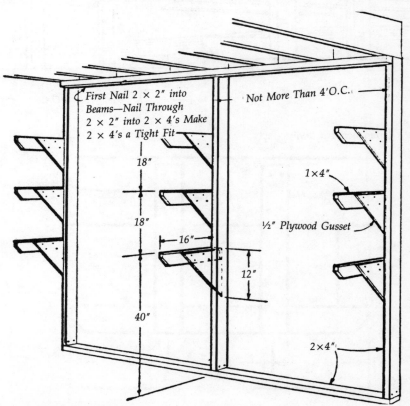

Fig. 4-1. Wall-mounted lumber rack.

Ceiling Rack
4 pieces   2″×4″×24″
2 pieces   1″×4″×43¼″

Wall Rack
4 pieces   2″×4″×7′10⅜″
1 piece   2″×2″×7′10⅜″
9 pieces   1″×4″×16″
9 pieces   ½″ plywood gussets
              (4½ 1-foot squares cut in half)

**Table 4-1. Materials
List for Lumber Rack.**

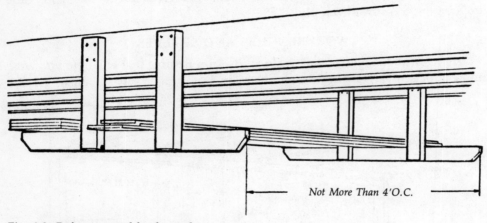

Not More Than 4′O.C.

Fig. 4-2. *Rafter-mounted lumber rack.*

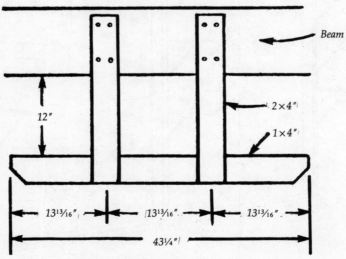

Beam

2×4″

1×4″

12″

13¹³⁄₁₆″   13¹³⁄₁₆″   13¹³⁄₁₆″

43¼″

Fig. 4-3. *Dimensions for rafter-mounted lumber rack.*

depends upon available space and work requirements. Some shops need no other work surfaces; others require space for a table saw, a frame for holding furniture to be repaired, and other fixtures.

Next come shelves. Solid shelves are vital if you plan to store numerous small parts or containers where they are readily accessible. Shelf support brackets are sufficient if all you are storing is long pieces of wood. Make sure that you can easily reach the objects on shelves without having to climb up on the workbench or a poorly placed ladder.

Pegboard walls are popular, especially when you need a number of tools displayed where they can easily be reached. Pegboard walls simply require a 2-×-4 frame attached to a solid wall or other unit, allowing sufficient space for hooks or pegs to be inserted into the holes. Tools and materials can then be installed on the hooks. In fact, special hooks can be purchased that are designed to hold specific tools: screwdrivers, hammers, fastener jars, wrenches.

With an efficient workshop you can dramatically reduce the time and increase the enjoyment of making easy weekend home improvements.

5

Panel a Wall or Room

Paneling is one of the most enjoyable home improvements you can accomplish in a weekend. The job usually proceeds quickly, especially if you have the correct tools, and makes a dramatic difference in the appearance of a room. You can add new color and tone by simply installing paneling on one wall, or you can dress up the entire room with paneling all round.

TOOLS AND MATERIALS

Tools for installing paneling are basic: hand or power saw with a fine-tooth panel blade, hammer, finishing or paneling nails, adhesive (if desired), touch-up sticks, and the panels themselves. You might also want trim to finish the job. Plan the job during the week and bring everything together so that, come a weekend morning, you're ready to go to work.

Most panels are 4 × 8 feet (48 × 96 inches) by ¼ to ½ inch. One person can move them, but it's much easier to have two. Run a rope from the left hand of the front carrier, underneath the horizontal panel, to the right hand of the back carrier.

PREPARING WALLS

Before installing paneling it is often necessary to paint ceiling, baseboards, molding, trim, and window and door casings. This is much easier to do before installing paneling than after.

If your walls are in good condition, you can glue and nail paneling directly into walls or studs, butting neatly against existing trim. On uneven, badly cracked, or very rough walls, panels can be nailed to a simple framework of 1-×-2 or 1-×-4 furring strips of any kiln-dried wood species and grade. Fitting shims (small wood shingles) under the strips will even up severe surface gaps. Furring strips can be installed either with nails or special wall adhesive in tubes.

To estimate panel and furring strip requirements, measure the wall width and length to determine how many panels you will need. You will also need to install furring strips around windows, doors, and other openings. You can fill the gap between strips with a thin insulating material to increase the efficiency of your heating system.

Then use a magnetic or electronic stud finder to locate wall studs. You can also estimate their location by finding a corner stud, measuring out 16 inches, and tapping the wall. Move your hammer around until you find a solid sound, which identifies the stud behind the wallboard. Mark the location of each with a pencil or snap line.

SELECTING PANELING

There is a wide variety of woods and other materials that can be used for paneling. Knotty pine, white pocket Douglas fir, sound wormy chestnut, and pecky cypress—real or simulated, finished natural, or stained and varnished—may be used to cover walls in a family room or recreation room. More formal rooms, such as the dining and living rooms, and master bedroom, can be enhanced with hardwood paneling in oak, maple, or elm.

Wood paneling should be thoroughly seasoned to a moisture content of about 10 percent. If it is installed too wet, it will contract as it dries, which could cause the wood or the finish to crack. This is true even of simulated wood panel finishes, because many use a low-grade wood or fiberboard backing. To ensure correct drying, place the sheets against the intended wall for a few days, allowing them to dry out on both sides. Don't stack them unless you lay furring strips between them to allow the air to circulate behind the panels.

INSTALLING PANELING

Panels can be applied horizontally or vertically, but the same general methods apply to both types of installation. Install using 5d or 6d casing or finish nails, or you can use paneling adhesive available in an application gun canister.

Match the first panel to the corner of what seems like the easiest wall to complete. Use your level to verify that the corner is plumb. Place and mark your first panel for any trimming you might have to do. If you must trim one side, do so on the side that fits into the corner, because the other edge probably has a rim that allows it to easily match the second panel. Once in place, plan how you will fasten the panel—with glue or nails—and consider where you will place them. Such mental planning might save you the trouble of having to take the panel down and start over.

Once you've set the first panel, the second will be easier. Remember to make cuts for windows, wall vents, and other openings before installing the paneling. To do so, measure the distance between the edge of the last panel and the opening, then mark it off on the back side of the next panel. Verify that it is correct, then make your cut. Some woods and tools require that you make your cut from the front side to reduce splintering. Take your time and you'll have a perfect fit.

Fig. 5-1. Installing horizontal solid lumber paneling (courtesy California Redwood Association).

Fig. 5-2. Nailing paneling (courtesy California Redwood Association).

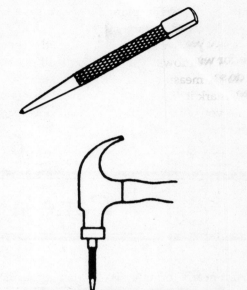

Fig. 5-3. Nail set.

Fig. 5-4. Using nail set to place finish nail head below surface.

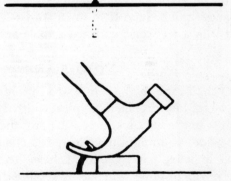

Fig. 5-5. Use a block to help pull bad nails while protecting the surface.

6

Cane a Chair

An art nearly forgotten is chair caning. Chair cane, a durable substance that comes from the rattan palm, is woven into the seats of wooden chairs, and gives strength, buoyancy, and beauty. If you're fortunate enough to have a cane chair, you can repair it in a weekend with basic tools and materials.

TOOLS AND MATERIALS

Rattan chair cane can be purchased through most upholstery supply stores and some larger fabric retailers. Typical width is ⅛ inch and length is 18 inches. Take a sample of the old cane, if possible, for the best match. If the replacement cane is too wide, you might have to redrill chair holes. For installation, you'll need an awl, a mallet, a wedge, and a chisel. You'll also need glue. If the cane is held in place with a spline, you should replace the spline. If it is strung through holes in the chair, you will also need a long weaving needle. Mats of prewoven cane can also be purchased, which makes the task much easier, but less challenging.

INSTALLING A CANE MAT

First, make sure that the cane holes or the groove is clear of dried glue, excess caning, or other materials that will make installation difficult. You might want to refinish your chair before recaning.

Prepare the rattan cane by soaking it in hot water for several minutes before installation. This softens the fibers and makes them less susceptible to breaking when installed.

Rattan cane mats can easily be installed by the do-it-yourselfer to replace an old chair seat or back. Once the chair is prepared, center the cane mat on the seat, making sure that it overlaps the area to be covered by at least 2 inches on each edge. Be sure that the pattern is exactly square before you begin. Spread a thin line of glue in the bottom of the groove. Tape one side so that it doesn't slip as you proceed with installation. Using a piece of wood slightly narrower than the spline groove, force the opposite side into the groove, from front to rear. Then remove the tape and do the opposite side of the chair. Finally, perform the same task on the front and rear grooves.

Once the caning is in place, use a chisel to cut it at the outside bottom edge of the groove. Then use the dowel and mallet to force the spline into the groove. Finally, allow the cane and glue to completely dry before using the seat.

Instead of using cane mat you might decide to weave your own cane to replace either strands or the complete chair seat or back. Preparation is the same: clear out the holes with an awl or drill, soak the cane until it is pliable, then begin weaving. Place the beginning of the first strand in a corner hole, hold it in place with a peg, and begin weaving from side to side, then front to back on top of the side-to-side strands. Now weave a strand from one side to the other going underneath the front-to-back strand. The second front-to-back strand alternates with the first. Finally, weave diagonally. Trim excess caning.

MAINTAINING CANE

Because rattan is a natural fiber, it requires little care to last many years. Cane can be periodically cleaned using a solution of salt and hot water. Rub it into the fiber, then rinse in warm water. Soap or detergent is not recommended. Blow or sun dry the cane to make sure that excess moisture is not trapped in the fiber.

Sometimes all an old cane chair needs is a little work. If it is stretched out of place, remove the seat frame including the cane, and soak it in warm water for 15 to 30 minutes. You might want to finish the bath with a mild washing, rinsing, and drying as outlined above.

7

Wallpaper a Room

Wallpaper offers decorative designs that painting cannot. Wallpaper can give a room a whole new look. A large design, for example, will make a large room appear smaller. A small pattern will create the illusion of more space in a small room. Two adjacent rooms can be made to appear more spacious by papering them in somewhat subdued tones, while a small, otherwise nondescript foyer can be given dramatic interest by papering it in a striking and vivid motif. And this can be accomplished on a weekend afternoon.

Wallpaper is becoming increasingly popular for ceilings, and not only in solid white, but patterns that compliment or reflect the walls. If you have a room with a high ceiling and painted walls, paper the ceiling in a soft design that matches the wall color. Run the paper about 2 inches down on the wall on all four sides of the room and finish off with a matching paper border. The result will be an attractive, well-proportioned room.

Closets, too, can be made more attractive with the addition of wallpaper. If the walls of the adjacent room are finished in a solid color, line the closets with a figure design in a matching or contrasting color. Even the door can be lined (but remember to remove knobs and fixtures first). If the closet has been painted in the same color as the room, wallpaper pasted to the shelves will add a unique touch.

PREPARATION

The rule of thumb for estimating wallpaper is: figure out the square foot area of the walls or ceiling to be papered, and allow a single roll for each 30 square feet of area. Because wallpaper comes in 36-square-foot rolls, the remaining 6 square feet can be used for trimming and matching.

When papering, repair holes and cracks in plaster as carefully as you would for a paint job. Hairline cracks don't have to be filled, but all open cracks must be repaired. Sand rough walls smooth.

INSTALLATION

You can use either self-adhesive or standard wallpaper that requires paste. Both follow the same installation procedures, except that sizing and pasting is not needed for the self-adhesive type.

Apply glue size when using standard wallpaper so that the glue can adhere to the wall. Sizing also stops surface suction, allowing the paste to remain wet long enough so that the paper can be moved slightly during hanging to ensure neat joints.

Remove light fixtures and switch shields, heating vents, and drapery rods before wallpapering. You can either remove trim around doors and windows or trim wallpaper where it butts the trim.

Wallpaper is usually hung from left to right around the room. If the sheets overlap, trim the left edge as needed. Measure the required lengths for the first three or four sheets, then lay them out on the floor or a table. Apply paste if needed. Carefully fold them so they do not stick to the pattern side or to the wall prematurely.

Mark the wall with a guideline to indicate where the edge of the first sheet should be. Verify that it is plumb so that wallpaper patterns will match properly.

Mount the ladder and unfold the top part of the strip. Fold down 2 to 3 inches at the top, paste to paste. Place the paper in position so that the folded top overlaps the ceiling slightly, and so that the right edge follows the guideline. Once in place, smooth the paper from the top down, in the center, with a smoothing brush. Then smooth to the right and left from center, halfway or farther down the wall. Make sure that the right edge is following the guideline.

At the bottom of the wall, crease the paper into the junction of the baseboard and wall. Then pull the crease away from the wall and cut with a pair of shears or a knife. Remove any paste from the woodwork before it dries. Continue hanging succeeding strips in the order in which they were cut. Match the first strip against the left edge of each strip and set accurately against the preceding strip.

Hint: to avoid buckling of paper in corners, cut the strip so that it overlaps the next wall by ½ to 1 inch. Hang the rest of the strip with as narrow an overlap as possible.

*Fig. 7-1. Set the plumb line
(courtesy Style-Tex).*

Fig. 7-2. Begin at the center of the room (courtesy Hyde Manufacturing Co.).

Fig. 7-3. Layout the wallpaper (courtesy Style-Tex).

Fig. 7-4. Apply adhesive with a roller (courtesy Style-Tex).

Fig. 7-5. Keep the water tray close to the wall (courtesy Style-Tex).

WALLPAPERING CEILINGS

To wallpaper a ceiling, carefully match the paper in one corner with one edge along your guideline, then begin unraveling it from the stack or roll. Use a round tube or pipe to assist you in holding the paper in place as you smooth it with

Fig. 7-6. Fold paper to the center for easier carrying (courtesy Style-Tex).

Fig. 7-7. Line up the first strip very carefully with the plumb line (courtesy Style-Tex).

Fig. 7-8. Brush and wipe to remove bubbles (courtesy Style-Tex).

the work brush. Continue brushing across the strip, making sure that wrinkles are taken out before proceeding. Then smooth and trim the joint between wall and ceiling. Continue with subsequent strips, using the previous strip as a guide for the next one. Be sure to match patterns as you go.

Fig. 7-9. Hang corners as shown
(courtesy Style-Tex).

Fig. 7-10. Use a seam roller
(courtesy Style-Tex).

Fig. 7-11. Trim carefully (courtesy
Style-Tex).

Fig. 7-12. Trim around receptacle
(courtesy Hyde Manufacturing
Co.).

8

Replace a
Decorative Light Fixture

A defective light fixture can easily be replaced by the do-it-yourselfer. Lighting fixtures usually come with their own instructions on installing the hardware and on making the right electrical connections, but most will use the following easy steps.

DISCONNECTION

The first step in any electrical job is to remove the circuit fuse or turn off the circuit breaker before doing any wiring. Merely switching off a switch on the wall won't keep you from being shocked. Always work with a dead circuit. Test to ensure that the circuit is truly closed by turning on or plugging in a light before disconnecting the circuit. This will give you visual proof that the circuit is dead.

You'll need a screwdriver, cutters, wrench, wire strippers, and a step ladder, as well as the new fixture itself. If you are installing a heavier light fixture, you might need additional support.

Disconnect the old fixture and remove it, carefully marking each wire as it is taken off the fixture. In most cases, the wire colors for the old fixture will match those on the new one, but not always. If in doubt, check the wiring diagram that came with the new fixture to determine the hot, neutral or ''common,'' and ground wires.

Inspect the house wires carefully for frayed covers, broken wire threads, and other signs of weakness that might cause problems. If necessary, run new wires as described in *Effective Lighting For Home and Business* by Dan Ramsey (TAB Book 1658).

INSTALLING FIXTURES

Use a wire stripper to strip the wiring cover on the new fixture back far enough to twist appropriate wires together, typically ½ to 1 inch. You might find three wires on the new fixture: a white neutral wire, a black hot wire, and a green or bare ground wire. Connect them to the appropriate house wires using twist-on wire connectors: white to white, black to black, and green to bare or the metal terminal box.

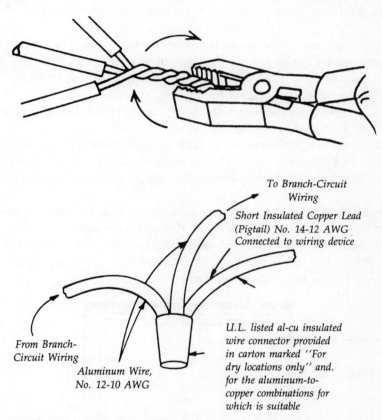

To Branch-Circuit Wiring

Short Insulated Copper Lead (Pigtail) No. 14-12 AWG Connected to wiring device

From Branch-Circuit Wiring

Aluminum Wire, No. 12-10 AWG

U.L. listed al-cu insulated wire connector provided in carton marked ''For dry locations only'' and for the aluminum-to-copper combinations for which is suitable

Fig. 8-1. Installing twist-on wire connectors (courtesy General Electric).

Once the wires are connected, mount the new fixtures using the hardware provided. Use either the mounting tab, the threaded nipple, or nut adapter to attach the new fixture to the ceiling box.

Before closing up the installation, turn the circuit on and make sure that the light works. Finally, carefully check over the connections, wire nuts, and terminal box, then install the wires into the box. Make sure that all parts are in place, then lift the lighting fixture itself into place and install the covers.

Check the area for any extra parts and the job is complete—congratulations!

INSTALLING LIGHT SWITCHES

You might have to install a new light switch with your new fixture. This is not a difficult task. The three most common types of light switches used in homes are single-pole, three-way, and dimmer switches.

When only one switch controls a light or wall outlet, you have a single-pole switch. They are the easiest switches to replace. First, remove any fuses or turn the circuit breaker off before doing any wiring. Remove the wall plate and the old switch, marking wires so that you can install the new switch in the same manner.

Wrap each stripped wire clockwise three-fourths of the way around the box screw. Alternatively, solid conductors may be inserted straight into a push-in terminal. Connect the ground wire to a green hex head screw, or fasten it to the metal box or metal switch bracket for proper ground.

Finally, mount the new switch in the box and replace the wall plate. Turn the power back on and test your switch.

A three-way switch always works with a second switch to control the same light, usually from the opposite end of the room or stairway. Notice that the three-way switch has three wires connected to the switch, while the single-pole switch has two.

In three-way application, only one dimmer is used; the other control must be an ordinary three-way switch. For safety, the dimmer bracket should be grounded. If the old switch has a ground wire (normally connected to the green hex head screw), fasten it to the metal box. If the box is plastic, fasten the ground wire securely to the metal dimmer bracket.

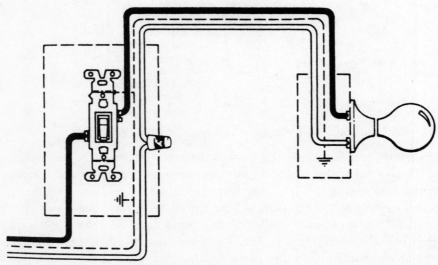

Fig. 8-2. Wiring diagram for a single-pole light switch.

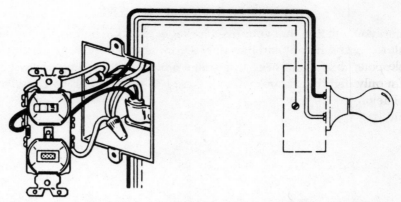

Fig. 8-3. Replacing a light switch with a dimmer switch (courtesy General Electric).

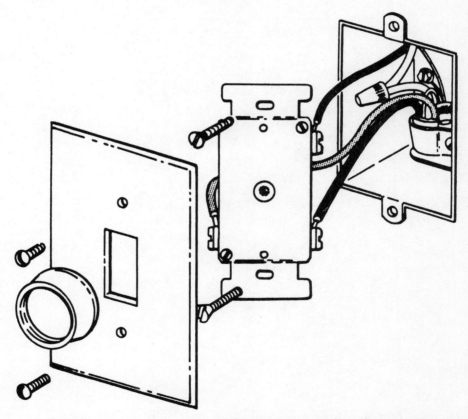

Fig. 8-4. Replacing a light switch with a switch-and-pilot-light (courtesy General Electric).

ADDING LIGHTING CIRCUITS

Sometimes you will find that your need for more electrical lighting has expanded beyond the point where it can be safely accommodated by your existing wire. If this happens, you might need to install a new circuit. Adding a new lighting circuit for your lighting fixture is more complex, but can still be completed as a weekend project.

9

Install a Bathroom Fan

You don't have to be an electrician to install a fan, heater, or other electrical apparatus in your bathroom. All you really need is knowledge of, and a healthy respect for, electricity. This weekend project will take you just a few hours, and will make a big improvement in your bathroom.

BASICS OF ELECTRICITY

Electric current can be compared to a current of water. The more current there is in a wire, the more light, heat, and power it will produce. The *ampere* or amp is the measurement of the amount of electric current flowing through a wire at any given time. Fuses, switches, and outlets are rated in amperes. That rating determines the size of the wire or cable needed for safe operation.

The *volt* is the unit of electric pressure that forces amperes of current to flow through the wires. The *watt* is the measurement of electrical power used. The amps multiplied by the volts gives the number of watts. For example, an appliance using 5 amperes at 110 volts will consume 550 watts. However, the watt is too small a measurement for most purposes; the kilowatt is preferred. A kilowatt hour is 1000 watts consumed over a period of one hour. Meters register power consumption in kilowatt hours.

Electric circuits are closed systems. Current runs through these from a power source to outlets where it is used, and back to the power source. In a series circuit, current passes through several outlets one after another, each taking from the current the amount of power it needs. However, if a light burns out or is removed, the circuit is broken. Most homes are parallel wiring circuits, so that one unused fixture or burned-out bulb does not shut down the circuit.

HOUSE WIRING

Your home is probably wired with either a two-wire or three-wire system leading into the house, depending largely on local electrical codes at the time the home was built. Many pre-1940 homes contain a two-wire system. In these, the white wire is neutral, and is probably grounded at the power panel by an attachment to the water pipe. The black wire is the "hot" wire. Both carry current; take care when working near them.

Today's homes are normally wired with the three-wire system, which provides both 115 and 230 volts—adequate for most home usage. In the three-wire system, two of the wires are hot and the third is neutral. The hot wires are usually black and red, while the neutral is white. All three feed into the main power panel, then branch out from there.

BATHROOM WIRING

Wiring in your bathroom provides power for lighting, heating, and ventilation. Your installation of a ventilating fan might be as simple as placing a manufactured bathroom fan into an existing outbound heating duct. Or it could be more complex, requiring that you mount the fan through a wall to the outside, or through a ceiling to an attic. You might even have to install ducting to the exterior before placing your fan. In colder climates, where a vent to the outside would allow chill to enter, you will want to vent the bathroom into an attic. This is easy to do in the only or top floor, but the main-floor bath of a two-story home might require ducting. Whatever the situation, talk to your local building material retailer about options, equipment, and materials before you begin making holes in the ceiling.

Once you've purchased the ventilation unit and determined its placement, make sure you can supply electricity. By plugging lights into wall sockets and turning on all installed lighting, you can find out what circuit breakers or fuses control which outlets and fixtures in your bathroom. Make sure they are off before you attempt any electrical work.

Make the hole for your vent. If available, use an electronic stud finder to locate studs, so that the unit can be installed adjacent to at least one stud for better support. Once the hole is made, determine the routing of the wiring from the switch to the fan. This is simple if you're replacing an overhead light with a combination light/fan. Otherwise, you might have to use a flashlight, a wire hook, and some imagination to run your wiring.

The instructions that came with the ventilating fan will show you how to hook it up using common electrical wiring practices. Screw nuts, often packed with the fan or purchased at your hardware, make connections easy. Make sure that you get the correct wires together. Once you're ready to install the fan into the hole, first have someone switch the power back on so you can test the unit to make sure it is wired properly. If you have any doubts, review the instructions. Finally, install the ventilation unit.

Installing an electrical heater or additional lighting in your bathroom is approached the same way: find out what's available, plan your job, respect electricity, then install it according to manufacturer's suggestions.

Additional information on installing ventilating fans, lighting, and heating is available in *The Complete Book of Bathrooms* by Judy and Dan Ramsey and Charles R. Self (TAB Book 2708).

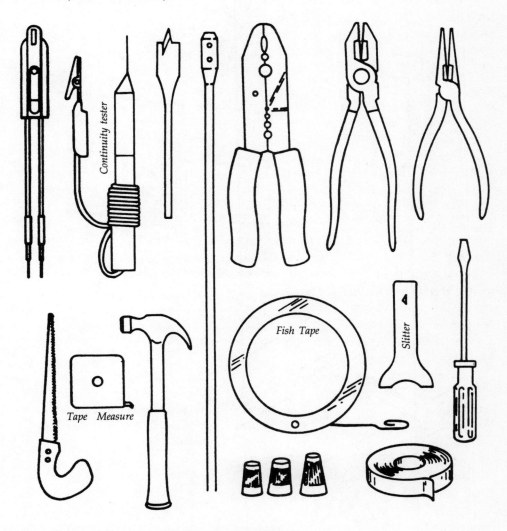

Fig. 9-1. Home wiring tools (courtesy General Electric).

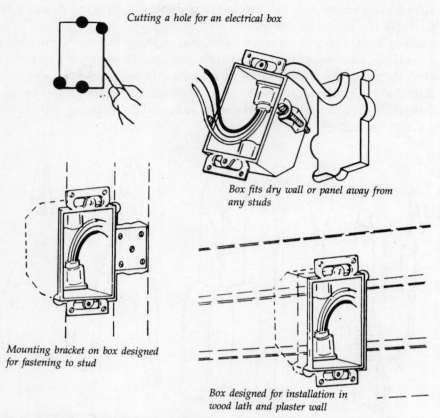

Cutting a hole for an electrical box

Box fits dry wall or panel away from any studs

Mounting bracket on box designed for fastening to stud

Box designed for installation in wood lath and plaster wall

Fig. 9-2. Mounting an electrical box in the wall (courtesy General Electric).

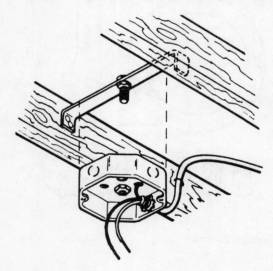

Fig. 9-3. Mounting an electrical box in the ceiling (courtesy General Electric).

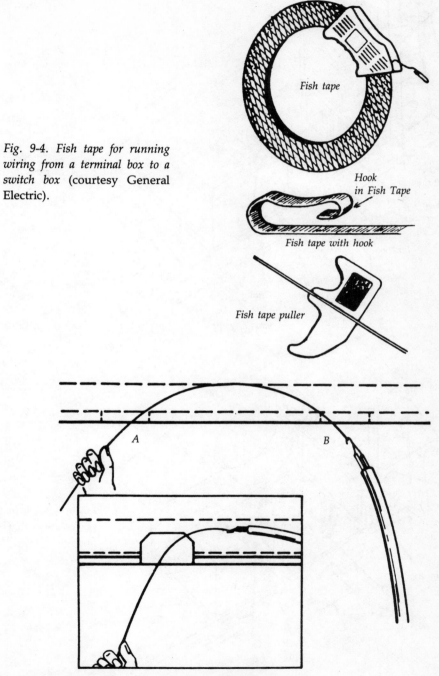

Fish tape

Hook
in Fish Tape

Fish tape with hook

Fish tape puller

Fig. 9-4. Fish tape for running wiring from a terminal box to a switch box (courtesy General Electric).

A

B

Fig. 9-5. Using a fish tape (courtesy General Electric).

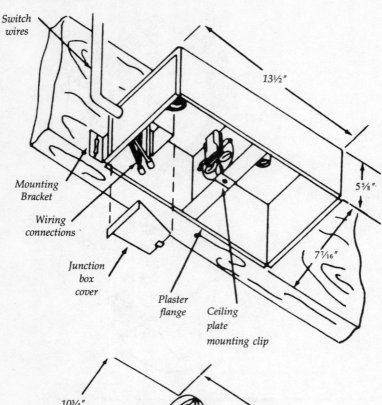

Switch
wires

Mounting
Bracket

Wiring
connections

Junction
box
cover

Plaster
flange

Ceiling
plate
mounting clip

13½"

5⅝"

7⁷⁄₁₆"

*Fig. 9-6. Mounting the box
(courtesy NuTone).*

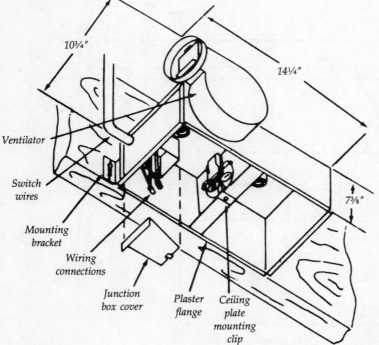

10¾"

14¼"

7⅜"

Ventilator

Switch
wires

Mounting
bracket

Wiring
connections

Junction
box cover

Plaster
flange

Ceiling
plate
mounting
clip

*Fig. 9-7. Installing the fan
(courtesy NuTone).*

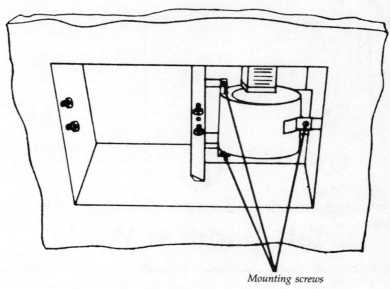

Mounting screws

Fig. 9-8. Mounting the fan (courtesy NuTone).

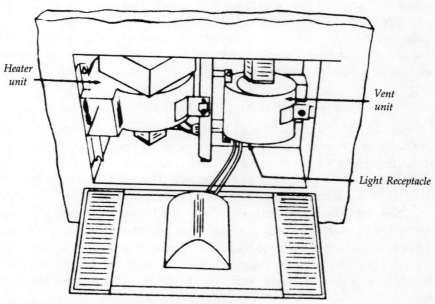

Heater unit

Vent unit

Light Receptacle

Fig. 9-9. Mounting the light (courtesy NuTone).

10

Install Bathtub Walls

For many years, the only way to enclose a bathtub into a shower was to line the walls with ceramic tile and install a shower curtain and bar. The project was time-consuming and required skills that many do-it-yourselfers didn't have. Therefore, many homes didn't have showers above the tub.

Today, modern plastics have made the task of constructing bathtub walls so easy that even the inexperienced home mechanic can select and install them over a weekend, at a cost of about $100.

TOOLS AND MATERIALS

Tools for installing bathtub walls are basic: hammer, saws, screwdrivers, caulking gun, and any special tools needed to remove the old wall, if necessary.

Materials include a bathtub wall and/or shower door kit, adhesive, waterproof caulking, nails, and the walls or door themselves. There are numerous types and brands of bathtub walls available, often on sale, at building material retailers. However, it's best not to select the least expensive unit because thin walls of inferior plastics will soon crack and leak, making replacement necessary. It is wiser to select a unit that is in the middle to higher cost range, depending on your budget. In the case of sliding doors, the framing and materials for so-called budget units are often poor and more easily broken, leading to a potentially dangerous situation.

PLANNING

First, determine whether you will be installing a three-wall unit, a sliding shower door, or both. Then you can attempt to match the styling and colors of existing and new units and trim to enhance your bath.

The next step is to take careful measurements of the area in which the units will be installed. Measure the width, height, and depth of the tub, sketching the results out in top and front views on graph paper. With this information you're ready to go shopping.

For better selection and price, it's best to shop for bathtub walls at a larger building retailer—one that offers at least a few units installed in a showroom. It's difficult to imagine how the unit will look in your bath if it's still in the carton. In addition, you can often get a sales clerk to show you the step-by-step procedures for installation right in the showroom, which will help you to make the best decision.

There are two common types of bathtub wall units: three-piece and five-piece. Which you select depends on your own tastes. A five-piece is slightly more difficult to install, but is more practical in a tub area where walls aren't completely plumb and corners aren't square. Make sure the sliding shower door is the correct size and of sufficient strength to allow for the some abuse.

While you're at the building materials retailer, select the appropriate caulking and other materials you might not have.

INSTALLATION

The first step to installing your bathtub walls is to prepare the existing walls. In some cases, this might require simply cleaning them off and repairing any holes. In other cases, you will want to remove the old tiles and install a ¼-inch underlayment panel to ensure a smooth surface. Remove old soap dishes and towel racks, and cover any large holes they leave.

To install a sliding shower door, prepare the bathtub lip and the walls for attachment of the tracks and rails. If you are dropping the ceiling above the tub to the top of the sliding door, verify locations and frame in the soffit now.

Follow the manufacturer's instructions for installing your new bathtub walls and/or sliding shower door, making sure that all parts are included before proceeding. Basically, the corner units are installed with waterproof adhesive spread using a caulking gun. Make sure that they are plumb, then install the wall unit(s) between the corners. Once in place, allow the adhesive to dry as directed. First lay the shower door track, then plumb and install the wall tracks. Install the top track and slip the doors into place. The top should be put in the track, lifted, and then the bottom set into the appropriate track. Set the door in the farthest track first.

Finally, caulk the walls and door with waterproof caulking. You can select caulking in a color that will accent your decor. If you haven't caulked before, spend a few minutes practicing: Spread the caulk in a joint, wipe it out, and try again. Once you have some experience, caulking will go smoothly. Make sure you haven't left any bubbles in the caulking, especially on lower surfaces where water can seep behind the tub or walls and damage the underlying wall. Take a few more minutes to carefully inspect your job and make any minor additions or repairs.

11

Replace an
Interior or Exterior Door

Doors are handy gadgets that allow the world into your home on your own terms. And if it's time to replace one, you can do this easily in one weekend.

DOOR TYPES

There are three types of interior and exterior door designs: batten, panel, and flush. The batten door is easily constructed, and is often used for vacation hideaways, sheds, and other basic structures. Most homes use panel and flush factory-built doors. The panel door consists of solid vertical members called *stiles*, solid cross members called *rails*, and filler *panels*. The flush door is typically constructed using a wood frame covered by a panel. These are used mainly on closet and storage rooms.

Interior and exterior doors are constructed differently. The typical interior door is 1 ⅜ inches thick, while the exterior door is 1 ¾ inches thick. Factory-built hinged doors come in standard widths of 18, 24, 28, 30, 32, 36, and 40 inches. Front doors are commonly 36 inches wide to allow for the entry of large furniture. Other exterior and most interior room, stairway, and basement doors are 30 or 34 inches wide. Double-entry doors are available in 60-, 64-, and 72-inch widths. Standard door height is 6 feet, 8 inches; variations range from 6 feet, 6 inches to 8 feet. Doors without hinges come in a wider variety of widths and sizes.

DOOR REPLACEMENT

Replacing a door that doesn't require a new frame is a very simple job. Planning the task might take more time than actually doing it. Replacement doors can be purchased with standard hinge locations. You simply remove the old hinge, and block the new door open so you can easily install the hinge on the frame. Make sure it is plumb. To make the task easier once you're sure the door and hinges will fit without modification, knock out the hinge pins and install the half-hinge squarely.

Prehung door replacements for the entire door and frame take a little more work, but are still a weekend morning or afternoon job. First, protect your finish wall and trim, then run a razor blade around the perimeter of the trim before you remove it. This will give you a clean break from your paint or wallpaper. Then carefully remove the interior door trim and save it. Remove the existing hinge pins, then remove the old door from the opening and set it aside.

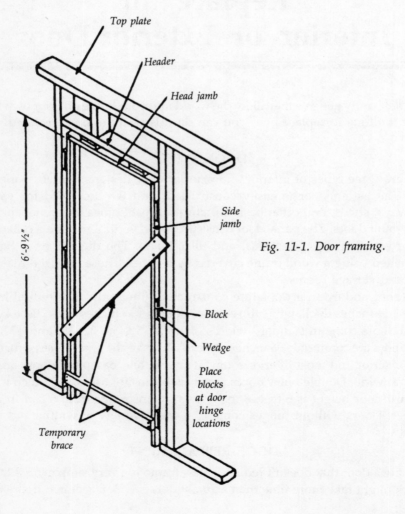

Fig. 11-1. Door framing.

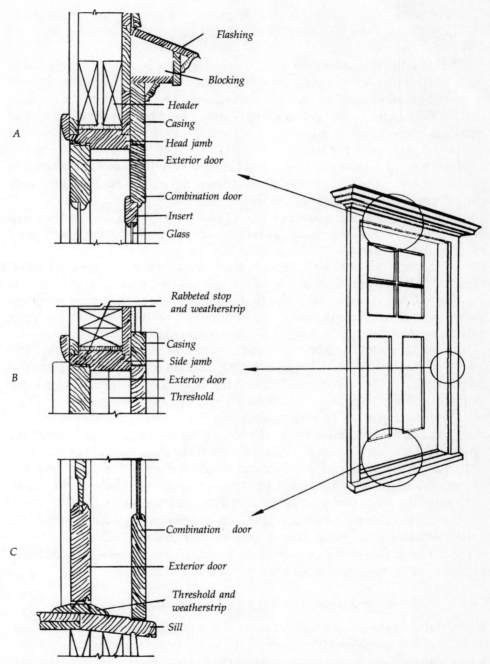

Fig. 11-2. Exterior door and frame cross sections: (A) head jamb, (B) side jamb, and (c) sill.

Next, remove the screws and hinge plates, the existing lock strike plate, weatherstripping, and threshold—if any. Make sure that the opening is square and the sill is level.

Position the replacement door in the opening. Don't cut the shipping bands yet because they keep the unit square and make installation easier. Use a pencil or masking tape to mark the location of the door sill on your floor. Lift the door unit back out of the opening. Measure 3¾ inches from the interior sill guideline and mark the exterior sill guideline, parallel to the first. This guideline will aid in placing caulking beads later.

Sweep away surface dirt from the sill area and carefully apply two beads of caulk. Make sure the caulk is about 1 inch inside the interior scribed line. Caulk completely around the sides of the jambs.

Place shims as needed between the old jamb and the lock area on the frame of the replacement door with a ¼-inch lath stock. This will prevent forced entry by spreading the jambs.

Set the replacement door in the opening, being careful not to smear the beads of caulk. Shift the unit slightly toward the lock side to ensure that the lock will be secure. Use a level to make sure that the hinge side of the unit is plumb to the face of the wall in the opening. Nail through six predrilled holes on the hinge side of the metal flange, but don't nail them into place yet.

Adjust the lock side frame in or out until it is flush with the opening. Use a level to check that the lock side is plumb, and shim as necessary. Now you can nail through the six predrilled holes in the lockside of the metal flange. Once in place, cut any shipping bands from the replacement door.

The next step is to drill three ⅛-inch pilot holes through the jamb and into the stud, one at each hinge. Install the screws, torqueing them down until the heads are flush with the hinge surface. Do not make them too tight or the frame will be distorted. More sure that the head margin is even and correct. Open and close the door to check for smooth operation. If it rubs or binds on the frame, tighten the top hinge screw. Once the door operates smoothly, secure the frame.

If your door doesn't include a lockset hole, drill two ⅛-inch pilot holes through predrilled holes in the frame. Torque screws down until the heads are flush with the lock frame. Open and close the door to make sure it meets the lock frame properly. Make the necessary adjustments, and you're done.

SOLVING INSTALLATION PROBLEMS

If you test your door and it doesn't make contact, the frame might be wracked. The solution is to drive nails on through the lock jam and correctly align the lock jamb with the door so that the weatherstripping meets the door evenly. Weatherstripping will compensate for up to ⅛ inch of wracking.

If the side jamb is uneven, shim the lock jamb until the margin between the door and jamb is even, top to bottom (approximately the thickness of a half-dollar).

If the head jamb seems too wide or the bolt and strike are misaligned, the unit is out of square. Shim the bottom of the hinge jamb or adjust the shim behind the top hinge.

If the side jamb margin is too wide from the top hinge, the weight of the door has pulled a bow in the jamb above the top hinge and below the bottom hinge. The solution is to use long screws in the top hinge to pull the door to the hinge jamb. An additional shim might then be required at the bottom hinge. Both of these corrections will help to restore the proper margin on all four sides of the door unit.

12

Refinish a Wood Floor

A new hardwood floor offers rich, deep beauty unsurpassed by vinyls, carpet, or tile. Finishes enhance the natural wood grain and protect wood from stains and abrasions for many years.

Unfortunately, time and use can wear the finish on hardwood flooring until the original beauty is nearly gone. Many homeowners decide to carpet over hardwood flooring rather than refinish it. However, the cost of refinishing is often less than the cost of quality carpeting. A do-it-yourselfer, renting a floor sander and applying a finish, can do the refinishing for less than $1.00 per square foot. A floor refinishing contractor will charge $1.25 to $2.00 per square foot, depending on the finish used.

Some homeowners have solid hardwood flooring in their home and don't realize it. The low cost of hardwood flooring just a few decades ago made it a popular subflooring for carpeting. Acquiring a new hardwood floor might simply be a matter of removing the carpet and finishing or refinishing the floor below.

FLOOR PREPARATION

Before new flooring is finished or old refinished, hardwood floors should be checked to make sure that boards are tight, cracks have been filled, and serious defects removed. If stains or burns go too deep for easy removal by sanding, the board should be replaced before finishing. Also remove any base shoes.

SANDING

An electric floor sander is a necessity for this job. As noted earlier, you can either rent one or have a contractor handle this part of the job. Forget hand sanding

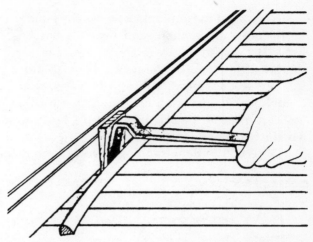

Fig. 12-1. Before sanding an old floor, remove the base shoe (courtesy National Oak Flooring Manufacturers Association).

Table 12-1. Sanding Guide for New Floors.

FLOOR	OPERATION	PROBLEM	GRADE OF SANDPAPER	
Hardwood		Uneven Floor	Medium-Course	2 (36)
Oak, Maple,	First Cut	Ordinary Floor	Fine	1 50
Beech, Birch	Final Sanding		Extra Fine	2/0 (100)
		Uneven Floor	Medium-Fine	1½(40)
Softwood Pine	First Cut	Ordinary Floor	Fine	1 (50)
Fir	Final Sanding		Extra Fine	2/0 (100)

or using a small belt sander. You will spend days per room sanding by hand. If you do decide to rent a machine, keep in mind that they require skill to operate safely. You might want to begin your sanding job in a large closet or in an area where large furniture will later be placed, so errors will be covered. You'll also need an edge sander to sand up to the molding where the large electric floor sander can't reach.

The first step to refinishing your hardwood floor is, of course, to remove all furniture and sweep the floor completely clean of surface dirt. Don't attempt to wash the floor, because the remaining moisture will affect your sanding.

Next, sand the entire floor across the grain using coarse sandpaper. Use the large floor sander, then sand near the baseboards with the edge sander. Be especially careful not to gouge the wood or leave low spots. This is especially important for some of the newer ⅜-inch hardwood flooring.

The second, third, and fourth sandings are all done with the grain. Use medium, fine, and extra-fine sandpaper for these sandings. The dust bag will pick up most of the sawdust, but it's best to remove draperies because finer sawdust will settle in them.

Once you're done sanding, sweep the remaining sawdust away.

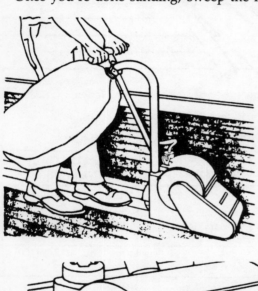

Fig. 12-2. Floor sanding machines can be rented at large rental centers (courtesy National Oak Flooring Manufacturers Association).

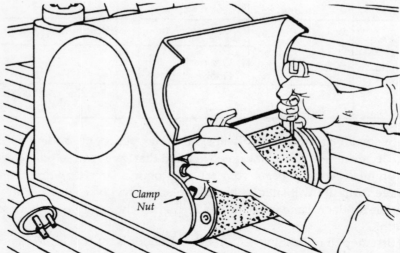

Clamp
Nut

Fig. 12-3. Drum-type floor sander (courtesy National Oak Flooring Manufacturers Association).

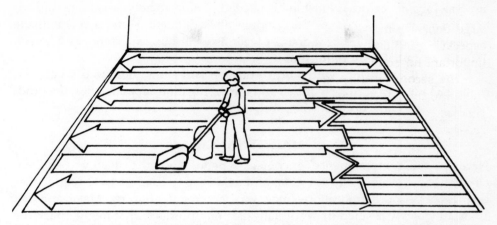

Fig. 12-4. Sand in the longest direction of the room (courtesy National Oak Flooring Manufacturers Association).

Fig. 12-5. When done, reattach trim (courtesy Harris-Tarkett).

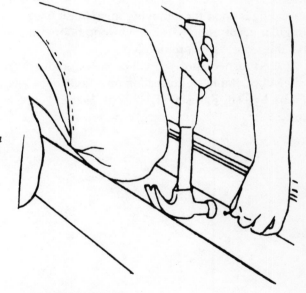

REFINISHING

There are a variety of hardwood floor finishes available, depending on what type of surface you would like. Hardwood floors can be painted, varnished, shellacked, waxed, or covered with a polyurethane finish. Older floors were varnished or shellacked, then waxed. This required heavy maintenance with weekly, and sometimes daily, buffing.

The most common hardwood floor finishes today are oil-based and water-based urethane. Oil-based urethane is the most popular and, if maintained, will last 5 to 10 years before refinishing is needed. Unfortunately, it is more difficult to refinish small areas, because the coloring will be different. Water-based urethane is easier to spot apply, but it doesn't wear as well. Life expectancy is between 4 and 8 years between refinishing.

Spread floor finishes with a brush or mop and allow them to dry between coats. The number of coats required and the drying time depends upon the product; follow the directions on the label.

MAINTENANCE

Hardwood floor maintenance, of course, depends upon the finish you applied. Urethanes can be cleaned with water and mild soap. Waxed surfaces require wax cleaners, a periodic application of new wax, and regular buffing. Make sure that spills are quickly cleaned up, especially cleaning products that might attack the finish itself.

Dirt and sand are the enemies of the floor's finish. Sand under a person's foot acts just like the sandpaper that you used to remove the old finish. Dust mopping is good for removing dust, but it usually doesn't pick up sand and dirt. Regular vacuuming with a hardwood floor attachment (a small unit with a brush on the front) is recommended.

A refinished hardwood floor can offer low-maintenance beauty to your home.

More complete information on refinishing a wood floor is available in *Hardwood Floors* by Dan Ramsey (TAB Book 1928).

13

Remodel a Recreation Room

Most homeowners look forward to the day when they can remodel a spare room into a recreation room. Too often, however, the work is postponed because they feel that it would be either too difficult or too expensive to do. Actually, taken a step at a time, it is neither difficult nor expensive. In fact, you can start this weekend.

LAYOUT

First, decide on the best location for your recreation room. If one of the rooms of the house can be spared for this purpose, the decision becomes much easier. Remember, though, that recreation rooms are likely to be noisy, and should be cut off as much as possible from the rest of the family activities. The attic or the basement are usually the best locations. In both of these locations, space is frequently wasted, so with a little ingenuity and skill these can be made over into rooms that greatly enhance family comfort and pleasure. And of the two, the basement is probably preferable, because it is more convenient. If neither the attic nor the basement is available, you might be able to convert part of a large garage. In this case, however, you will probably first need to install heating, lighting, and convenient access.

Once the location has been chosen, the next step is refurbishing the walls and ceiling. If they are unfinished, they may be paneled with any one of many composition materials now on the market: plywood, wallboard, plasterboard, fiberboard, or veneer paneling (see Project 5). If the recreation room is to be in the attic, it will be well worth the time and expense necessary to insulate the ceiling and sides of the room. After all, a recreation room that is either too hot or too

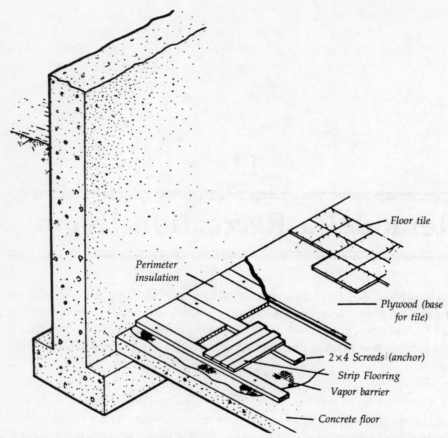

Fig. 13-1. Remodeling a basement recreation room often requires that you insulate floors and walls.

cold to be enjoyed will get little use. If you live in a rather mild climate, rigid insulation board will provide adequate insulation. In most cases, however, a blanket or batt type of insulating material fastened between the studs will give much better results.

In planning the layout for the room, consider using partial partitions or sectional walls that extend into the room. If space is limited, these walls can be built for storage as well as for divisional purposes. If the room is large, they will set off the various activity centers and utilize space better.

The next step is to provide a suitable floor covering. If the present floor is reasonably smooth, you might not need a new floor. Otherwise, consider installing a resilient tile floor.

The organization of the room will be determined largely by its major activity. If it is to be a game room with a ping-pong table and other large pieces, the rest of the furniture will be grouped accordingly. All of it should be sturdy and well-built to stand up to hard knocks and rough usage. On the other hand, if the chief center of recreation is to be the card table or a conversational group of easy chairs, you will probably arrange the larger part of the available space for this purpose. However you plan to use the room, be sure to provide one or two secondary centers of interest for the enjoyment of those not actually engaged in the major activity.

Adequate lighting is very important. The design and arrangement will, of course, depend on the room's activities. A large game or card table obviously should have a good overhead light. Other parts of the room can be illuminated by well-placed floor and table lamps. Fluorescent lights are especially useful in a recreation room; they give a bright and diffused light without glare. Light troughs that provide concealed and indirect lighting will give your room a modern look. Additional information on lighting is offered in *Effective Lighting For Home and Business* by Dan Ramsey (TAB Book, 1658).

A good activity for this weekend is to sit down with family members and decide what you want included in your new recreation room. How often it will be used depends upon whether family members consider it ''their room,'' as well as its proximity to the main living area.

Also consider the changes your recreation room will make in the coming years. An active family with young children playing cars on the floor quickly becomes one with teenagers playing pool with friends, then one where empty-nest parents play cards every week with a club. With careful planning, your recreation room can serve many needs over many years.

Spring Projects

14

Build a Cold Frame

Sooner or later, every serious gardener finds a cold frame almost a necessity. Not only can it be useful for starting seedlets in the spring, and for developing delicate plants, it is also handy for extending the productive season of many vegetables. Imagine enjoying fresh salads a month or more later into the season than you do now.

The purpose of a cold frame is to shelter the plants against cold. A cold frame is actually no more than a four-sided box, covered with glass on a hinged sash. The side walls may be made of wood, concrete, brick or any other durable material. Wood is the material most commonly used and is the least expensive. However, for maximum durability, the lumber should be redwood, cypress, or other close-grained wood, at least 1 inch thick. It is best to first select your sashes, then construct the frame to fit them.

LOCATION

You must find the proper location in order for the cold frame to function properly. Ideally, it should be shielded from the weather, so it is best installed near a wall or fence. It should also be oriented so that it receives a maximum amount of sunlight. Place the cold frame as near the garden as possible for easy transfer of plants.

Excavate the spot where the frame is to be set to a depth of 12 to 18 inches, then fill in the bottom with a layer of cinders and a layer of topsoil. The surface should be 12 inches or less from the top of the frame. Plant beds, cold frames,

Fig. 14-1. Basic coldframe.

Fig. 14-2. Attached greenhouse.

and small greenhouses built well below the level of the ground require less heat than those that are entirely above ground and more exposed. Make sure, however, if you install your cold frame bed partially below ground, that the location offers good drainage during rainy seasons.

CONSTRUCTION

The size of the cold frame will vary according to the needs of the gardener. For most purposes, a frame 36 × 72 inches with a 12-inch front board and a 15-inch back board is sufficient. Two 36-×-36-inch standard window sashes can serve as the top. However, select those that allow easy drainage of water that collects on the glass. The sashes should be hinged at the back, with a center strip installed on the frame for them to rest against when closed. Screen door hooks will allow the sashes to latch to a wall or fence when the unit is open.

Assemble the frame around corner 2 × 4s driven firmly into the ground. Extra 2 × 4s, driven down at the center outside about midpoint of the long sash, will prevent the frame from spreading. Use scrap pieces to prop open the sashes for ventilation.

Construct a shutter that fits over the top of the sashes. This will serve as shade for sensitive seedlings and will protect the glass when the cold frame is not in use.

HOT BED CONSTRUCTION

Hot beds are much the same as cold frames, except that other provisions are made for heating them beside the warmth of the sun. The most common kind of hot bed is one heated by manure under the topsoil. In building this bed, sink the walls deep enough to put down a layer of about 15 inches of manure with 6 inches of topsoil over it. Another means of heating the bed is by placing it near a basement window, which can be opened to allow the warmth from the basement to enter the frame.

15

Fence a Garden

There are many good reasons to install a fence around your garden: most of them have four legs, some just two. A well-constructed fence can secure your veggies from those who would share your harvest without permission.

It's not difficult to fence out most small animals, raccoons being the notable exception. All you need is a fence that they cannot go over, under, or through. A 4-foot high, 2-inch mesh poultry wire fence buried 1 foot into the ground is often sufficient. Livestock and most people can be kept out with a 4- to 6-foot barbed wire fence.

PLANNING

Your garden fence should contain your plot, but also allow you to easily enter and exit with equipment. Of course, it should also allow the sun to enter. Measure out your garden, allowing space for planned expansions, and mark the dimensions on your garden plan. Determine your access point and requirements, and decide whether you will need a full gate or just an opening.

There's a law for just about everything, and fences are no exception. Fence laws are usually practical: don't build a fence on someone else's property, don't build a fence where it will obstruct the safe view of drivers, and don't build a fence that will detract from the value of neighboring properties. Before you actually construct your garden fence, check your title insurance policy to see if there are any restrictions that might apply. Check for utility easements; fences can't be built on most easements without written permission from the holder. Contact the county or city building department to determine what regulations they might have. Some have basic regulations and a small fee based on the fence's value.

If your garden fence is a seasonal structure, the requirements might be waived, but it's always best to check first.

Once your fence is planned, check around for scrap materials that could help reduce the cost of your garden fence. You might already have old fence posts, lumber, metal, or rolls of fencing that can easily be used.

CONSTRUCTION

Materials you need for garden fence construction include posts, metal fabric or wood slats, and fasteners. The most popular fencing for gardens requires steel posts and woven wire fabric.

Steel posts offer a number of advantages. They are lightweight, fireproof, extremely durable, and easily driven into most soils, all of which simplify installation. Steel posts are usually sold in lengths from 5 to 8 feet, in increments of 6 inches. The most popular is the 6-foot post that is driven 2 feet in the ground to hold 48-inch wire fabric. Make sure that you have checked the area, or had it checked, for utilities. Quite often, underground utilities are buried near a property line, which is also a favorite location for gardens.

When you install your garden fence, first place the corner posts. Anchor them well, because they will receive the greatest strain. They can be anchored in concrete, gravel, or solid ground. However, you might want to crossbrace them with a turnbuckle to ensure that they do not bend under the load. Install line posts 4 to 8 feet apart, depending on the size and weight of the fence.

There are various classes of woven wire fencing. These include stock fencing, poultry or garden fencing, chicken fencing, and wire netting. Your local building supply or farm supply store can help you select the best type for your application. Basically, though, wire fencing is sold by the *gauge* and the number of line or horizontal wires. The lower the gauge number, the larger, stronger, and more costly the wire. The stay (vertical) wires in the fencing are usually of the same gauge as the filler (intermediate) wires. They may be spaced 6 or 12 inches apart.

Most woven wire fencing is either zinc-coated (galvanized) or aluminum-coated. Chain link fencing is available with a vinyl resin coating. Galvanized fencing is classed as 1, 2, or 3. The class number, shown on the fencing's roll tag, indicates the fence's galvanizing. Class 3 typically has at least twice as much zinc as Class 1. The coating on aluminum-coated fencing is usually about 0.25 ounce per square foot of wire surface.

Woven wire fence fabric is installed by attaching one end to a corner post and stretching the fabric to another corner post. This is best accomplished with a fence stretcher. Make sure that you don't overstretch the fabric. This could damage the corner post, or worse, cause the fabric to snap back and hit you. Once this is done, you can attach the fence securely to the line posts using clips on the steel posts or U-nails for wood posts. You can also install a line or two of barbed wire at the top of the fence to discourage climbers. Your fence should only be electrified if you are trying to keep livestock out, and there is no danger of humans touching it. Electric fences develop enough voltage to stun a cow; imagine what it can do to a young child.

For more information, read *Fences, Decks and Other Backyard Projects* by Dan Ramsey (TAB Book 2778).

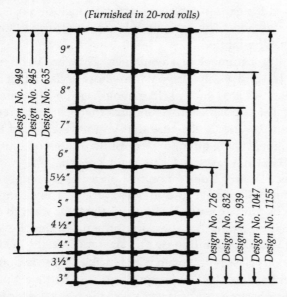

(Furnished in 20-rod rolls)

Fig. 15-1. *Horizontal wire spacing for different designs of woven wire field fence.*

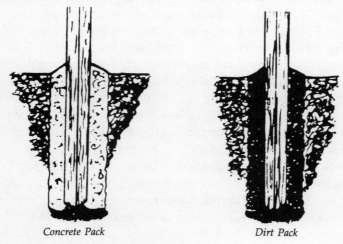

Concrete Pack   Dirt Pack

Fig. 15-2. *Concrete pack and dirt pack postholes.*

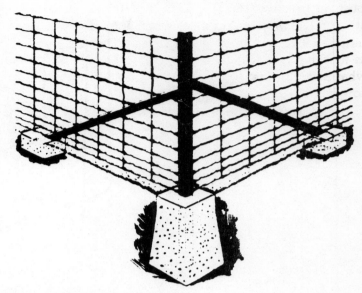

Fig. 15-3. Supporting a corner post for a large fence.

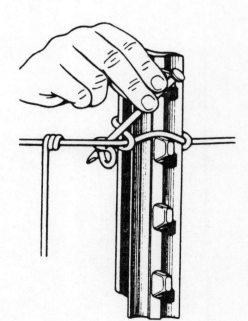

Fig. 15-4. Method of applying a steel post wire clip.

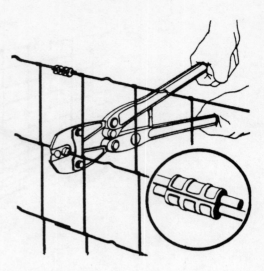

Fig. 15-5. Compression sleeve for splicing wire.

16

Build a Storage Shed

Utility building kits are great. They design the structure, gather materials and fasteners, offer step-by-step procedures, and almost guarantee you good results. They are also more economical than the individual components that you buy. One of the easiest outdoor structure kits to construct is the utility building or storage shed. It can easily be constructed in a weekend, depending on how fancy you want to make it.

The 8-×-8-foot storage shed kit described here uses special plates that set the correct angle as well as fasten framing members together.

CUTTING COMPONENTS

First cut the base segment. Take one member that is 8 feet, 2 × 4 inches and make a pencil mark on one edge, at a point 4 feet from one end. Next, take a plate and place it on the face of the 2 × 4 so that the apex is even with the mark. Position the plate so that the top edge of either arm is flush with the outside edge of the 2-×-4 segment. Holding the plate firmly, mark through each cutting slot. Remove the plate and mark a cutting line through the marks.

Using a square, mark a line across both edges of the 2 × 4 from the ends of the cut line. This will help you make an accurate cut and joint. Cut the segment, and you will have a template for the remaining vertical base members.

Cut the rafter frame segment. Note that there are angle cuts at each end. Both angles are the same, with one opposing the other. Mark off on a 2 × 4 a length 2 feet 7 ½ inches. Position the plate so that the apex is even with the right mark, and the top edge of the left arm of the plate is flush with the outside edge of the 2 × 4. Using the cutting slots, plot the cutting line.

Fig. 16-1. Typical storage shed (courtesy Georgia-Pacific).

Fig. 16-2. Combination shed-greenhouse (courtesy Georgia-Pacific).

At the left end of the 2 × 4, position the plate so that the apex is even with the mark, and the top edge of the left arm of the plate is flush with the outside edge of the 2 × 4.

Mark square lines across both edges at both ends of the rafter segment to ensure an accurate cut and joint. Cut the segment, and you will have a template for the remaining rafter segments.

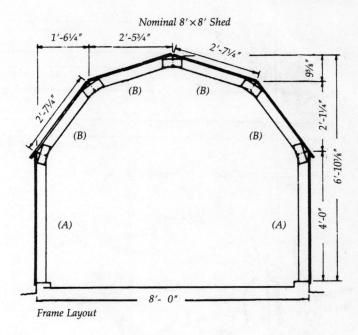

Nominal 8′ × 8′ Shed

1′-6¼″   2′-5¾″   2′-7¼″

9⅝″

(B)   (B)

2′-7¼″

(B)   (B)

2′-1¼″

6′-10⅞″

(A)   (A)

4′-0″

8′- 0″

Frame Layout

Fig. 16-3. Plans for an 8-×-8-foot shed (courtesy Teco).

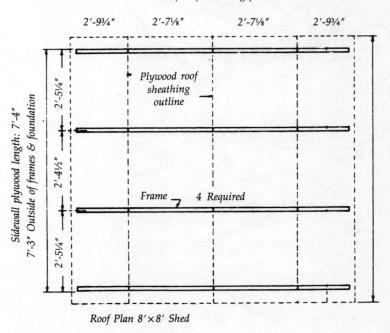

Width of roof sheathing panels:

2′-9¾″   2′-7⅛″   2′-7⅛″   2′-9¾″

Sidewall plywood length: 7′-4″
7′-3″ Outside of frames & foundation

2′-5¼″

Plywood roof sheathing outline

2′-4½″

Frame   4 Required

2′-5¼″

Roof Plan 8′ × 8′ Shed

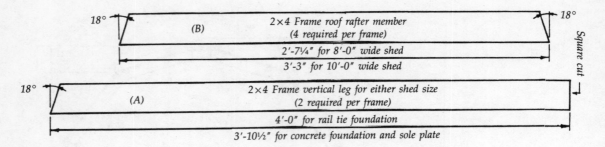

18°   2×4 Frame roof rafter member   18°
        (B)   (4 required per frame)
                        2'-7¼" for 8'-0" wide shed
                        3'-3" for 10'-0" wide shed

Square cut

18°   2×4 Frame vertical leg for either shed size
        (A)   (2 required per frame)
                        4'-0" for rail tie foundation
                3'-10½" for concrete foundation and sole plate

Fig. 16-4. Cutting shed members (courtesy Teco).

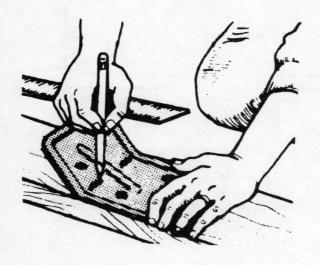

Fig. 16-5. Marking members
(courtesy Teco).

Fig. 16-6. Bolting shed construction plate (courtesy Teco).

ASSEMBLY

Assemble the vertical base. Place a plate on the 2-×-4 segment so that the cutting slots line up with the angle cut at one end of the segment. Make sure that the top edge of the plate is flush with the outside edge of the segment. With the plate in this position, make a starter hole for the drill by tapping the thread end of a ⁵⁄₁₆-inch bolt through the hole in the plate and into the wood. Still holding the plate in position, use a portable drill with a ¹¹⁄₃₂-inch bit to drill through the hole in the plate.

Once the hole has been made, slip a ⁵⁄₁₆-inch bolt through the plate and into the wood to help hold the plate in position while the second hole is drilled. Make sure the plate is in position during drilling. Then insert a ⁵⁄₁₆-inch bolt and apply a plate to the other side of the joint by inserting bolts and applying nuts. Hand tighten nuts at this time.

Drill the next adjoining segment, which will be one of the rafter members. Place one end of the rafter segment so that the end cut fits snugly against the matching end cut of the adjoining segment. Then place the top edge of the plate flush with the outside edge of the segment. Make a starter hole for the drill as you did previously.

Hold the joint tightly together with the plate in proper position. Make sure the drill is perpendicular to the boards. Put the end of the drill bit through the hole in the plate and drill an ¹¹⁄₃₂-inch bolt hold through the board.

Next, insert a ⁵⁄₁₆-inch bolt to help hold the segments in place. Drill the second bolt hole, following the same procedures as before, and apply nuts to bolts on the other side of the plate. Continue drilling and making joints around the rest of the frame until all have been assembled. Don't fully tighten the bolts with a wrench until you have checked that the bottom ends of each vertical leg are 8 feet apart.

An alternate method is to use nailing plate fasteners at joints. This is easier, but it might not be as sturdy.

CUTTING PANELS

Before erecting the end frames, use one of the frames as a pattern to plot cutting lines for end panels. Do this by laying two 4-×-8-foot panels side by side, flat on the ground. Place a frame on top of the panels and mark around the outside of the frame. You can also cut the intermediate framing members comprising the end frame and door frame at this time.

ERECTING FRAMES

The end frames are erected first as shown in the illustrations. Drive two stakes about 2 feet out from the frame. Cut two 2 × 4s long enough to reach from the

Fig. 16-7. Erecting and paneling shed (courtesy Teco).

stakes to the top of the side vertical segments. Nail one end of each 2 × 4 to each stake. Then, using a level, plumb the frame and nail the 2 × 4 braces to the frame. Erect the frame at the other end of the shed following the same procedure.

Nail side panels to the end frames using 6d nails. Mark locations of the inside frames on the side panels. Nail 1½-inch angles to the bottom of each upright segment, place the frames on the base, and nail the angles in place. Nail the side panels to the sides of the frames using 6d nails.

Cut the roof panels to measurements shown in the diagram. Install the top roof panels first, then the lower units using 6d nails. Finally, finish your shed with roofing, paint, and hardware.

Refer to *Fences, Decks and Other Backyard Projects*—2nd Edition by Dan Ramsey (TAB Book 2778) for additional information on storage sheds and other outdoor buildings.

17

Install a Garage Door Opener

The modern family with a two-car garage and two or more cars soon finds that a garage door opener would greatly simplify things. A garage door opener can easily be installed in a weekend with just a few ordinary tools.

The tools you'll need include a hammer, screwdriver, wrench, measuring tape, drill, saw, and a stud finder. Unless you play professional basketball, you'll also need a ladder. Your garage door opener kit will include most of the materials you need: the unit, screws, clamps, and brackets. You'll also need nails, 2-×-4 wood for framing, and one or two batteries.

PLANNING

First, measure the height and width of the garage door. This is important because the size and type of door will dictate which door opener you purchase. You need a more powerful door opener for a heavy double door than you would for a light single door. You also need a minimum clearance of 2 inches between the door and ceiling for space to install your garage door opener.

Determine whether you have a one-piece swing-up or sectional roll-up garage door. Inspect your garage door to make sure that there are no mechanical problems that will prevent smooth action and possibly damage the opener's motor. If the door, frame, or track needs repair, do it now. Lubricate all tracks and wheels.

INSTALLATION

Most garage door openers operate by pulling the top of the door along a ceiling track toward the back of the garage. Reversal allows the garage door to slowly fall back into the closed position. Make sure your garage door opener can easily be reversed.

Measure across the top of the inside door frame and mark the center point, which should be directly above the handle. Install the header bracket exactly over this mark and at least 2 inches down from the ceiling, or as recommended by the manufacturer. Install the header bracket with screws. Next, install the hanger straps or crossmember onto which the opener unit will be installed. If the ceiling in your garage is sheetrock, use a magnetic or—preferably—an electronic studfinder to determine the exact location of studs for supported installation. If the ceiling is exposed beam perpendicular to the door, you can easily mount the unit on the side of a roof rafter.

Once installed, you need to bring power to the garage door opener. Most openers simply plug into a socket and need no wiring. Run a wire and outlet from the garage electrical box to within 12 inches of the garage door opener unit. First make sure, of course, that the unit's cord is at least 12 inches long—modify it to suit. Complete instructions on electrical wiring and outlet installation are offered in *Effective Lighting For Home and Business* by Dan Ramsey (TAB Book 1658).

The opener's track is easier to install if you have a helper and a second ladder. Set one end of the track into the header bracket above the garage door and loosely bolt it into place. Install the other end on the hanger straps or rafter straps. Then install the garage door opener unit in place, if you haven't already done so. Install the lifting bracket on the door itself, the carrier into the track, and the connecting arm between the bracket and carrier.

Most garage door openers require additional wiring inside the unit in order to operate. This might mean simply connecting up wires, or programming the opener's code. In any case, carefully follow manufacturer's instructions, because all units will be somewhat different, depending on type and features. Finally, replace the cover on the unit and plug in the garage door opener.

Before testing the opener, take a few minutes to inspect the installation. Have all bolts and screws been tightened completely? Is the track straight and level? Have you tested your electrical outlet? Have you lubricated moving nonelectrical parts? Have you installed batteries in the remote unit? Check manufacturer's instructions on what type and number of batteries to install.

To test the unit, simply push the button to make the garage door open and close a few times. Do this from inside the garage so that you can carefully watch its operation. Try opening and closing with both the wall unit and remote unit. You might have to make minor adjustments to the track and connector arm, but, if the unit binds, quickly pull the plug to the outlet switching off the motor.

18

Install Attic Ventilation

An attic ventilation system can keep your home cooler, and, if you have an air conditioner, save you money during the hot summer months. It can also lower heating costs by reducing condensation in the attic. And here is more good news: Installing an attic ventilation system is an easy weekend project.

During cold weather, a warm attic that is inadequately ventilated and insulated can cause ice dams to form at the cornice. After a heavy snowfall, heat causes the snow next to the roof to melt. Water running down the roof freezes on the colder surface of the cornice, often forming an ice dam at the gutter. This could cause water to back up at the eaves and into the walls and ceilings. Similar dams often form in roof valleys. Ventilation provides part of the answer to these problems. With a well-insulated ceiling and adequate ventilation, attic temperatures are low, and the melting of snow over the attic space is greatly reduced.

In hot weather, ventilation helps remove hot air and lower the temperature. Free circulation of air is important in making a house comfortable during the hot months. To accomplish this, leave the attic windows open and allow the air to move up from the lower parts of the house and escape through the windows. The overheated air in the attic can flow out, thereby drawing the air from the room below. If there is no window in the attic, you can install a louver without much difficulty.

PLANNING VENTILATORS

There are several ways to move warm air out of an attic. If the space is entirely enclosed and has no windows at all, the simplest method is to install louvers or vents near the ridge line of the roof. These vents should be placed in opposite gables so that air can circulate freely between them. They are constructed much the same as a window, except that slats are placed across the opening to slope downward at a 45-degree angle. This arrangement allows a free flow of air while keeping out the rain. Build the louver frame so that a tight-fitting screen can be attached to the inside to keep out insects and bats.

With correctly sized and properly installed ventilation, the house can be cooled by several degrees during the summer. Permanent or portable exhaust fans can further improve ventilation.

Types of ventilators and minimum recommended sizes have been generally established for various types of roofs. The minimum net area for attic ventilators is based on the projected ceiling area of the rooms below. The actual area must be increased to allow for any restrictions such as louvers and wire screens. The screen area should be double the specific net area.

Fig. 18-1. Triangle vent.

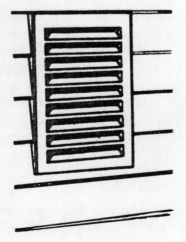

Fig. 18-2. Wall louver vent.

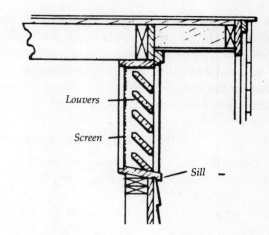

Fig. 18-3. Vent cross section.

Fig. 18-4. Soffit vent.

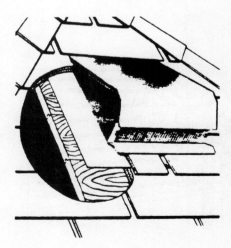

Fig. 18-5. Hip roof vent.

Louvered openings are often constructed in the end walls of gable roofs, close to the ridge. Hip roofs should have air inlet openings at or near the peak. The most efficient type of inlet opening is the continuous slot, providing a free opening of approximately ¾ inch. Flat roofs require even more ventilation than gable and hip roofs because they offer less circulation. In most cases, these ventilators can be installed in overhang soffits.

INSTALLING VENTILATION FANS

To increase the flow of air, you can install a fan at the louver or window. Ventilating fans are either wind-powered or electrical. If yours is wind-powered, make sure to install it below the roof ridge line so that it does not become too active when winds run up the face of the roof.

Electrical ventilating fans are usually easy to install on the inside of the ventilator. They typically run on 110-volt electricity and are best turned on and off by a covenient light switch. For easiest installation, use an existing attic light that has a downstairs switch. Wire the fan parallel with the light, placing a chain-pull socket at the light as an on-off switch that won't interfere with the circuit to the fan.

Specifics on wiring can be found in *Effective Lighting For Home and Business*, by Dan Ramsey (TAB Book 1658).

SAFETY

Last, but certainly not least, remember that a forced circulation of air through the air is dangerous if fire breaks out. For this reason, close the ventilating system and shut off any fan before going to bed.

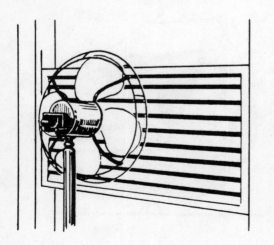

Fig. 18-6. Installing a portable fan in front of a vent.

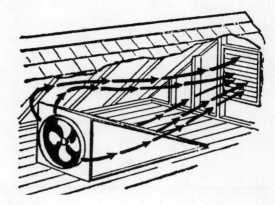

Fig. 18-7. A larger fan can circulate more attic air.

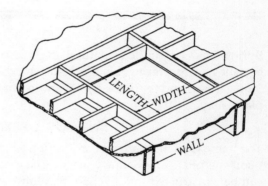

Fig. 18-8. Framing in a fan.

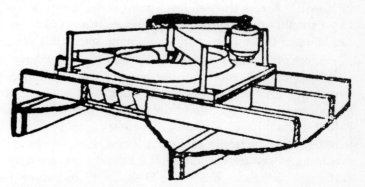

Fig. 18-9. A large permanent attic fan can dramatically increase the cool air within your home.

19

Install Plant Shelves in a Window

Spring has sprung. The natural urge to plant something and watch it grow becomes overpowering. Here's an idea for those who don't have the time or space for a garden, and for those who want to prestart their garden indoors: a window plant shelf.

INDOOR GREENHOUSE

The home gardener can use early spring sunlight to start plants indoors by adding plant shelves to an existing window that gets plenty of sunlight. A growing space can be constructed in a kitchen, breakfast room, basement, or even a garage in some climates.

Along the length of the windows, build a long counter that is supported on top of a wood frame. Allow sufficient depth to hold the amount of soil that will be needed. Across the windows themselves, attach a bracketed shelf on which to set small potted plants for exposure to the sunlight. The undercounter space can be used for storing spray equipment, gardening cans, and other materials.

Select the location that will best add to your enjoyment and convenience. Consider not only sunlight, but also overhead lighting, running water, floor covering, proximity to an outside door, and potential hazards. Consider the temperature of the room and the kinds of plants that you wish to grow. If the room faces south and has a broad expanse of windows, a good part of the daytime heating will come from sunlight. In some cases, you might even want adjustable screening to reduce the sunlight, so plants are not damaged y overexposure. Automatic adjusters are best. They open and close vents and shading to compensate for temperature changes, and maintain a nearly constant environment for best growing conditions.

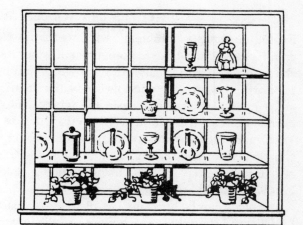

Fig. 19-1. A deep window can easily become a plant window.

Fig. 19-2. Construct a plant shelf and bed in your gardening center.

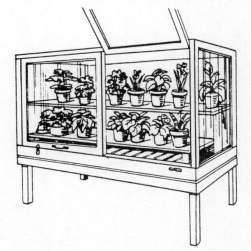

Fig. 19-3. A small greenhouse can be placed in front of a south-facing window.

SHELVES IN PROBLEM WINDOWS

Every house has a "problem" window that just doesn't seem to fit the general architecture of the house. Sometimes it is set too high on a wall, or is an odd shape, or it proportionally throws the room off balance. If it faces any direction but north, this problem window can be the site of your new window greenhouse.

If it isn't necessary to open the window too often, you can install shelves permanently in the window. To do this, decide how many shelves you want. Then mark off the window frame at the proper heights on each side, and nail short pieces of quarter-round molding to the frame as shelf supports. You can also install partial shelves, using shelving brackets that are available at the hardware store.

Shelves can be specially cut plate glass, plastic, or wood. Glass is the best for allowing sunlight to reach plants on the lower shelves, but it is also the most expensive.

WINDOW BOX

Whether you have only one small sunny window or a group of windows in a bay, you can build a window box that can bring the fragrance and color of living plants to your home. The box can be a simple extension of the window sill, or a more elaborate arrangement with a cupboard space underneath for storage of indoor gardening paraphernalia.

The window-box cupboard is construction that resembles the old Pennsylvania sink, with the top of the cupboard flush with the window sill and the sink about 6 inches deep. You might have an old sink left over from a remodeling job, or you can purchase a used porcelain or metal sink and build a cabinet to fit around it. The cupboard can easily be built of plywood, with a single or double door hung

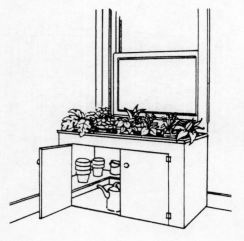

Fig. 19-4. An old sink cabinet can easily be modified into a window box.

using simple hardware. Line the bottom of the cupboard and attach hooks to the walls so you can store tools and materials below.

If you prefer to enjoy rather than tend plants, consider those that require less care. A cactus and rock garden makes an interesting window display that rarely needs attention, but still offers natural beauty.

MANUFACTURED GREENHOUSE WINDOW

Sometimes the best solution for the do-it-yourselfer is to let someone else do the hard work. This is especially true for constructing a greenhouse window. These are units that replace your current window, and protrude out to catch as much sunlight as possible. Better units include a cranking ventilation system, adjustable shelving, and a high insulation factor to minimize heat loss.

When shopping for a greenhouse window, first measure your selected window. Draw a plan of the current window on a sheet of graph paper, marking all dimensions. You can easily estimate the actual size of the window opening by measuring the casing and adding the thickness of the window frame. Take these measurements to your building supply retailer or window shop. They can help you determine the best unit to fit your requirements. Because it is a home improvement, the addition of a greenhouse window can often merit a low-interest loan from your bank, if needed. This is much cheaper than charging it to a bank card.

Because installation is unique to each unit, make sure you get an instruction sheet with the unit. Ask if you can get installation support from the retailer, if someone can help you with questions.

20

Build a Concrete Walk

Installing or repairing a concrete walk is an easy, but labor-intensive weekend project. "Labor-intensive" means that you will sweat. The following instructions will guide you in replacing a portion of your current sidewalk, or installing a new one.

PLANNING

First, check local building codes for specifications and requirements for concrete walks in your neighborhood. Most sidewalks are 4 to 5 feet wide and about 4 inches thick for normal traffic. The sidewalk's greatest enemy is water. Where drainage is poor, the concrete should be poured over a 6-inch cinder or gravel fill. Sidewalks are constructed so that they will drain. Most are $3/8$ to $5/8$ inches higher on one side than the other, which prevents water from gathering in pools. An alternative to sloping a walk is to level it, when the concrete is hardening, with a strike board that has a slightly concave curve, not more than $1/2$ inch deep. This produces a $1/2$-inch ridge or crown in the walk, which will shed the water.

The sidewalk's second greatest enemy is trees. Install your concrete walk as far as possible from large trees.

TOOLS AND MATERIALS

The tools you'll need to build a concrete walk include shovels, a hoe, pails, a measuring box, mixing platform, a heavy tamper, a strike board, a wood float, an edger or groover, a hammer, and a saw. Tools you don't have can either be rented or borrowed.

Materials include sufficient cement, aggregates (rocks), and water to make enough concrete for the sidewalk (or you can use ready-mixed concrete); lumber for constructing forms; heavy felt; stakes; and spreaders. You might also need cement compounds and burlap to control the drying process.

CONSTRUCTION

The first step to building a concrete walk is to dig a trench deep enough so that the surface of the walk will be about 2 inches above the surrounding grade, regardless of whether a sublayer is used. Dig the trench about 1 inch wider than the walk will be, so that stakes can be driven into the ground.

Next, tamp the bottom of the trench smooth and level. Place 2×4-inch pieces of lumber along the sides of the trench. Drive stakes at 4-inch intervals on the outside of these boards to hold them in position.

At standard intervals, usually every 4 to 6 feet, place spreaders into the form. The spreaders should be as long as the sidewalk is to be wide. Stake, don't nail, them into place. Cover the face of each spreader with a strip of heavy, tarred felt. normally, a thicker ½-inch spreader is installed every 25 to 50 feet, and at adjoining curbs.

Now, mix the concrete based on specifications furnished by the manufacturer and your building materials retailer. Pour the concrete into alternate sections of the form and screed, or smooth, the concrete with the strike board. Allow each section to stiffen sufficiently to be worked with a wood float, making sure you don't eliminate any crowning. Then use an edger or groover to round off the tops of the cracks in the walk.

Let the concrete harden and remove the spreaders. Then repeat the steps for the remaining sections. Allow the concrete to cure for a week to 10 days by covering with burlap or wet straw. The concrete must not be allowed to dry too quickly. After curing, carefully remove the forms and fill the joints with a mastic or Portland cement compound. Cover the top of the joint with a thin Portland cement paste, and groove lightly before it sets. Finally, build up the surrounding grade to the edge of the sidewalk by replacing grooves on either side of the walk with dirt excavated from the trench. Wet and tamp the dirt, then replant lawn seed.

BUILDING A BRICK WALK

A brick walk is easy to build, and attractive and interesting designs can be made with the bricks. Such a walk is a handsome addition to any home or garden. Brick walks have an advantage in that the bricks can be put down in a bed of sand without the preparation cement requires.

Carefully mark the pathway to the desired width, and cut the sides down vertically. The typical brick is about 2 ¼ inches thick; consequently, the path should be dug at least 3 ½ inches deep. This will allow 1 ½ inches for a sand foundation, and the bricks will rest only a fraction of an inch above ground level. When you have made the excavation, roll or tamp earth at the bottom of the path, and make it as even as possible by adding or removing soil. Then add the sand and level it.

Place the bricks as close together as possible, and use a board or line to get each course straight. After the bricks are in place, pour sand over the walk and sweep it into the joints between the bricks. Spray the walk with a garden hose, using the fine spray to pack the sand down in the joints.

Additional information on cement and forms can be found in *The Complete Foundation and Floor Framing Book* by Dan Ramsey (TAB Book 2878).

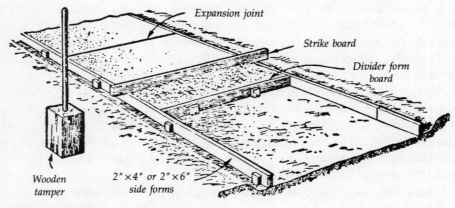

Fig. 20-1. *Making a concrete sidewalk.*

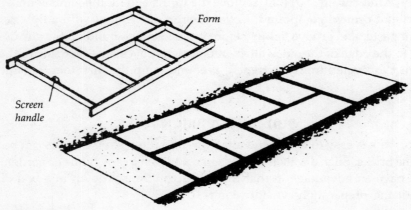

Fig. 20-2. *Flagstone walk.*

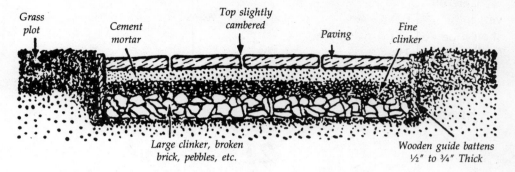

Grass plot

Cement mortar

Top slightly cambered

Paving

Fine clinker

Large clinker, broken brick, pebbles, etc.

Wooden guide battens ½" to ¾" Thick

Fig. 20-3. Cross section of garden path.

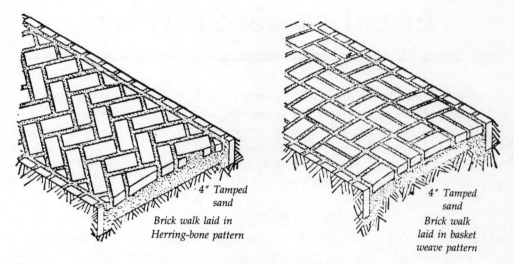

4" Tamped sand

Brick walk laid in Herring-bone pattern

4" Tamped sand

Brick walk laid in basket weave pattern

Fig. 20-4. Attractive brick walks can be built with bricks laid in a bed of sand.

21

Install Closet Shelving

There is seldom enough space in downstairs closets, particularly if your family is large or you live where heavy winter clothing are required. Too often, existing closets are cluttered and inconvenient simply because there is no place to put the odds and ends collected by family members.

An easy weekend project is to turn an inefficient closet or pantry into a well-planned storage space with shelving.

SHELVES

For strong shelving it is important to have boards that are stiff enough so they won't sag noticeably over the span required, and good support at the ends and at intermediate points.

Begin by measuring on the wall the position of the bottom face of the shelves. It's best to measure from the floor to the lowest shelf, then to measure off the shelves above from this line. End wall mounts are typically constructed of 1-×-1 or 1-×2 wood mounted to the wall with screws or nails. Exact mounting procedures depend on the type of wall you are attaching shelving to. For plaster or gypsum board walls, you will want to either anchor shelving to studs behind the wall or use anchor wings on the ends of bolts.

Brackets should be installed through walls and anchored into studs. Use an electronic stud finder or estimate stud position by tapping the wall with a hammer, searching for a change in sound that indicates the stud position. Hammer a thin finish nail through the wall to determine whether the stud is there. You can then measure off the standard 16-inch spacing between wall studs to look for the next stud. However, closet framing studs might be placed at closer distances, so verify stud location before you begin planning hangers.

Shelving can be made of a variety of materials: 1-inch pine lumber, tongue-and-groove lumber, particleboard, plywood, or sheets of plastic. Make sure that the material will support the intended weight. Obviously, a shelf for light bulbs requires less strength than one for canned goods. Whether you set your shelves on the brackets or install them permanently depends upon use. You might want to make them adjustable so they can be moved, according to seasonal needs. Or you might want the stability of reinforced supports and attached shelves (see Fig. 3-5).

CATCHALL CLOSET

Figure 21-2 shows how a pantry in an older home can be remodeled into a closet that serves many purposes. The top of the closet is fitted with shelves for

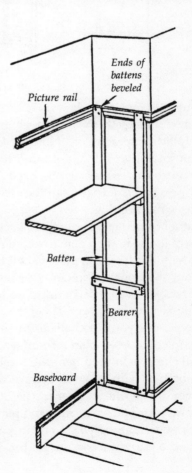

Fig. 21-1. Closet shelving installed in an alcove.

Fig. 21-2. Catchall closet.

infrequently used articles such as luggage, outdoor games, and seasonal equipment. Beneath these shelves are spots for everyday objects: coats, hats, shoes, play equipment, etc. Note the Dutch door that allows items to be retrieved without having to actually go into the closet.

Because this closet will be used to store mud-caked boots and shoes, wet overshoes, and children's sandbox toys, you will want an easy-to-clean surface, such as vinyl flooring.

Rather than dictate how this closet should be constructed, let's consider how you want to use it, then plan it accordingly. In sunnier climates, where overclothes aren't required, you can plan a shelf for picnic items that can be grabbed as you head out the door. In colder climates, you might want to add a shoe scraper, a boot rack, or even a small heater to help you change out of wet or cold clothing and into something warm. If you're a home mechanic, you might want to plan one portion of your catchall closet as a receptacle for tools and materials. Perhaps you could even plan a small workshop or sewing area into the unit. If the catchall closet is located near the washer and dryer, you might install a hamper in the bottom with a Dutch door at the top for placing clothes in sorting bins, and even install the washer in the other side of the closet.

Draw your plans out on graph paper, measuring the space you have and the shelves and hangers you want in your catchall closet. If the project requires widening a current closet or pantry, locate the studs and the wiring to ensure that your weekend project won't become a month-long chore. Buy as much of the components prefabricated as possible: doors, shelving, hook racks, hampers.

Once you have a materials estimate, take it and your plans to your local building materials retailer. Many will sit down and review your plan, suggesting ideas that can make it more efficient and less expensive. However, keep in mind that they are in business to sell. Don't buy more than you need. In fact, you might want to tackle your catchall closet in stages, installing additional shelving, hooks, and other components later as your budget allows.

Finish your catchall closet, or other shelving, with an enamel paint that will stand up to use. This is especially important if your closet is one designed for outdoor clothing and equipment. Easy-to-clean paint will add much to the efficiency of your catchall closet.

22

Install a New Sink

There are various occasions when you might want to install a new sink—when you're adding a bathroom or expanding your present bathroom, for example. You can select either a wall-mounted or cabinet-mounted sink. These instructions will show you how to easily install a new sink in a weekend morning or afternoon, and also how to remove an old sink.

TOOLS AND MATERIALS

Tools needed to install a new sink are basic: adjustable wrench, plumber's wrench, and a screwdriver. Depending on the installation, you might also need a hammer and a hole saw. You'll need a sink, faucet set, plumber's tape or putty, required piping, and a bucket.

REMOVING WALL-MOUNT SINKS

Until recently, the most common sinks were the wall-mounted units that actually hung from a bracket attached to a wall support. If you are replacing a wall-mounted sink with another one of the same style, you won't need to install a new bracket—unless it isn't sturdy enough to hold the new unit.

    The first step to installation is to turn off the hot and cold water lines to the sink. Depending on how much of the plumbing you are replacing, you might be able to just close the two shutoff valves located underneath the sink. The safest procedure is to turn off the cold water line coming into the residence and the hot water shutoff above the hot water heater. In many cases, the handles for these shutoffs are painted red for easy identification.

Next, place a bucket under the drain trap of the old sink. If the trap has a cleanout plug, remove it and allow the trap water to flow into the bucket, completely clearing the line so that you can work dry.

Wrap and loosen the slip nuts connecting the trap to the drain tailpiece and drain extension. Once loose, remove the entire trap unit, making sure that you also carefully disconnect the pop-up drain mechanism. Remove the drain trap.

The faucet is now removed. Use a plumber's wrench to loosen the locknuts at each shutoff valve. Because many of these are made of softer metals, be careful you don't damage them so that they cannot be removed.

With the sink now loose from the inlet and outlet lines, carefully lift the sink off the wall bracket. A helper can make sure that there are no dangling parts to make removal difficult. Set the unit down on a soft surface that won't be damaged by water.

REMOVING CABINET-MOUNT SINKS

Cabinet-mount sinks follow the same basic removal steps: shut off the water, clear and disconnect the trap, disconnect the shutoff lines, and remove the sink from the cabinet. In many cases, the sink is attached to the cabinet by a screwed-in rim retainer. If you are replacing just the sink, simply unscrew it from underneath and the sink will lift out.

The cabinet may be attached to the wall using Phillips-head screws installed through the back cabinet frame.

INSTALLING WALL-MOUNT SINKS

Depending on the installation, it is often easier to install the faucet on the sink before the sink is mounted on the wall. Using a soft surface and a wooden support, you can set the faucet gasket in place on the top side of the sink, push the water fittings through the sink holes, then add the washer, retaining nut, locknut, and water line from below. Take careful measurements to ensure that your water supply lines and drain tailpiece are of approximately the correct length before the sink is installed.

Once you have installed the wall bracket or are sure that the old one is correct and firmly installed, mount the new sink on the bracket. You might have to open the bracket up slightly and retighten it once the sink is installed.

Now attach the drain tailpiece to the drain fitting at the base of the sink, and tighten the drain flange locknut. If there is a pop-up drain mechanism, you can install it now as well. If not already in place, install the drain line extension that exits the wall. Then install the drain trap at the low end of the drain line, adjusting its position so that its horizontal end matches the drain extension line. Once you're assured that the lines fit together, seal and tighten them.

Attach the water lines from the faucet to the shutoff valves, and you're done. Place a bucket beneath the sink and slowly turn the water on to check for leaks. When you're sure that there are no leaks and that all fixtures are secure, you can begin using your new sink.

INSTALLING CABINET-MOUNT SINKS

Cabinet-mount sinks are installed in the same manner as wall-mount, except, of course, that you must also install a cabinet. However, the cabinet might limit placement adjustments, so you need to be especially careful when measuring the drain line and trap. Also, the cabinet makes it more difficult to reach some fittings. Plan your job out in advance, and remember not to fully anchor the cabinet until the plumbing is installed.

Additional information on installing sinks, faucets, and other fixtures is presented in *The Complete Book of Bathrooms* by Judy and Dan Ramsey and Charles R. Self (TAB Book 2708).

23

Install Carpeting

Carpeting is a newer floor covering that, for many years, was not considered a very good substitute for wood or tile. But with newer manmade fibers, lower costs, and easier cleaning, carpets have become the primary residential floor covering.

Whether you are installing carpeting for the first time or are replacing an older carpet, you can easily complete a room or more in a weekend.

TOOLS

To install your carpet you will need common as well as specialized tools. First, you'll need a measuring rule, hammer, nail set, screw driver, utility knife, putty knife, vacuum cleaner, and a paint brush. You'll also need a carpet stretcher or knee-kicker, which is available at your carpet store or through a rental shop.

Materials include carpeting, padding, adhesive, tacking strips, and staples. You can purchase all of these through your carpet retailer. In fact, many dealers will spend some time with you going over the procedures for installing carpeting. They would like to do the installation as well, but their primary concern is selling carpeting.

Some good advice from an expert carpet installer: Buy the better-quality padding. Even though it doesn't show, it is one of the most important components of your carpeting system. Good padding will not only make the carpet more enjoyable to walk on and use, it will also make the surface more resistant to rough wear.

BUYING CARPET

The first step to buying and installing carpet is to determine how much you need. Measure out your room from baseboard to baseboard and sketch it out to scale on graph paper. Mark the exact locations and widths of doors, radiators, fireplace hearths, and other wall interruptions. Then calculate the square yardage of the carpet you require: length and width in feet, divided by nine.

Carpet is usually sold by the yard in 9-, 12-, and 15-foot widths; padding is available in 4 ½-foot rolls. Tack strips come in 4-foot lengths and will run the perimeter of your room.

INSTALLATION

First, prepare the floor onto which you will install your carpeting. Move all furniture out of the room. Remove doors, floor registers, and other wall interruptions. Carefully remove molding and store it. Nail down loose flooring to remove squeaks. Make any patches necessary so that the carpeting can be installed over a smooth surface.

Nail down the tack strips around the perimeter of the room about ¼ inch from the wall, with their tips pointing toward the wall. This is important. Make sure that the fastening tacks are pointed down and the staples up before nailing them into place. Cut the strips as required to make corners. Use special thin strips at doorways.

With help, move the first roll of carpet into position and stretch it out in the room. Then fold half of it back to again expose the floor. Install the padding, waffle pattern up, over the floor to overlap the tack strips. Once the padding is in place, use the staple gun to fasten the padding to the floor every 6 inches around the perimeter. If you are installing the padding over a concrete floor, use adhesive instead of staples.

Once the padding is completely in place, run your utility knife around the edge of the padding to remove excess. The padding should run right up to but not overlap the tack strip. Cover the remainder of the room in the same way, rolling the carpet back over the area you just completed padding.

Now unroll the carpeting over the padding and carefully position it to overlap the tack strips. Trim the carpet carefully, allowing sufficient overlap at doorways; use a special doorway tack strip. Now, all that is necessary is to stretch the carpet into place.

Attach one end of the carpet to the tack strip on one wall to anchor it. Then stretch the carpet fabric toward the opposite wall with the knee-kicker. The knee-kicker grasps the carpet fabric with its brush-like surface while you make a quick kick to the padded end of the tool. Repeat this action across and along the carpet until any looseness in the carpet is worked out to the other wall.

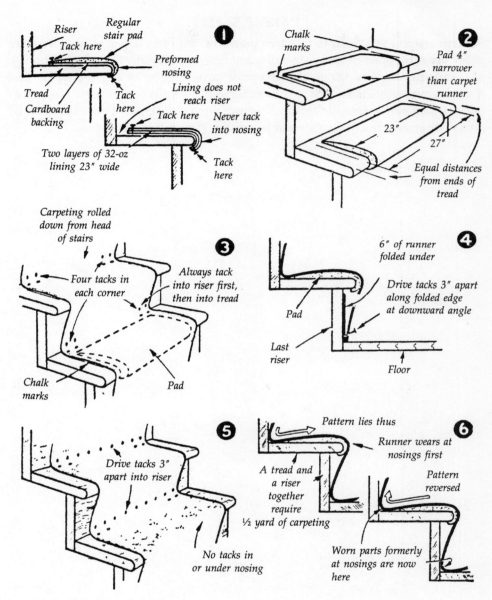

Fig. 23-1. Installing carpet on stairs.

Finally trim the excess from the carpet edges and push the ends of the fabric down into the ¼-inch crevice on the outside of the tack strip, using a putty knife. If you wish, the molding can be reinstalled, but many homeowners leave it off. Then install floor registers, doors, and your furniture.

CARPET SEAMS

Sometimes you will need to join two pieces of carpet in larger areas. There are a few ways this can be done. Install seam tape underneath the seam, then use a special seaming iron (available from your carpet retailer or rental shop) to seal it. Alternatively, install a tack strip or other jointing strip between the two pieces of carpet. In either case, do this before stretching the carpet. The seam must be joined carefully so it doesn't burst when the carpet is stretched.

24

Install a Bay Window

A dull wall can be brought to life with a decorative bay window. Bay windows can be added to nearly any style of residential architecture: ranch, gambrel, brownstone, Cape Cod, and even a mobile home. It will probably take you one weekend to learn how to select and install a bay window, and another to actually install it.

A bay window is a suitable addition to any room in the house—the living room, dining room, or hobby room—and is frequently used in an upstairs hallway. It is especially attractive in a dining room, because a small table set in the alcove of the bay creates a cheerful, sunny spot for the family breakfast. Bay windows are also becoming increasingly popular as a place for the indoor garden.

PLANNING

Materials used for the bay can be any of the usual building materials: wood, stone, or brick. The construction of the bay involves making adequate opening in the wall, providing sufficient structural support, and fitting the wall opening with a window unit that matches the lines of your home. Some do-it-yourselfers construct their own bay window, but the majority purchase a bay window unit selected to fit.

If the bay is to be added to a first-floor room and is to be set reasonably low in the wall, you should first install a base foundation for the window. This support should be firmly set on concrete or stone piers, and the floor and sides well insulated to resist cold, dampness, and insects. The roof over the bay should be similar to the roof style on the rest of your home.

Unless you have extensive building experience, adding a bay window to a second story should be left, at least in part, to a local building contractor.

The design of your bay window should harmonize with the general architectural design of the house. But the use of casement or louver windows, four- or six-pane windows, or stationary or sliding casements, is a matter of personal taste.

Fig. 24-1. *Bay window.*

Fig. 24-2. *Lower portion of bay window used for storage.*

INSTALLATION

The first step in installing a bay window in a wall is to lay out the opening between regular studs, if possible. Using a stud-finder, you can locate studs in an existing wall to determine exact placement of the window before you begin tearing into the wall. You will want to make sure that there are no plumbing pipes or electrical wires at your window location; if there are, they must be moved.

If might be necessary to move an existing stud or to add a new one. Make sure that the distance between the regular stud equals the suggested rough opening width of the bay window unit, plus the thickness of two regular wall studs (3 inches). Cut two pieces of header material—2 × 8s, 2 × 1, or 2 × 12s—equal to the rough opening width of the window unit, plus the thickness of two regular studs. Nail the two pieces of header material together so the header is as thick as a regular stud.

In most newer home construction, the header should be 6 feet 10 ½ inches from the subfloor. Position the header at this height between the regular studs. Nail through the regular studs into each end of the header to hold it in place until the next step is completed. Cut the jack studs to fit snugly between the soleplate and the header. Nail the jack studs to the regular studs and toenail them to the header.

The wall is now ready to receive your bay window unit. When the rough opening has been framed and found to be plumb and level, insert the bay window unit into the opening and allow it to reset on the rough sill to ensure a proper fit.

To prevent operating and weather-tightness problems later, check the window unit for plumb and level before fastening it to the opening. Check the window for level across the sill and head. Check for plumb two ways: side-to-side and front-to-back. To check for side-to-side plumb, use a carpenter's square at the corners of the unit, or check with a level at the side of the frame. To check for front-to-back plumb, place the level on the outside face of the frame to make sure the window is not tilted outward or inward.

To correct errors in plumb or level, use a pry bar to raise the sill of the window. When it's in position, drive a nail through the head flange into the rough framing member. If the sill is raised, be sure to shim the side to keep the jamb in a straight, plumb position. Check again for plumb and level, and nail the opposite corner of the window into the frame. Finally, check again for plumb and level, then completely nail the window into place. Metal window sashes are usually installed with screws rather than nails. Of course, follow the specific instructions packed with each window unit.

25

Install a Clothesline

Electric and gas clothes dryers have revolutionized the task of doing laundry. A load of washed and wet clothing is lifted out of the washer, slung into the dryer and a few buttons are pushed. Less than an hour later the clothes come out dry.

However, there are thousands of homemakers who annually return to the old standby, the clothesline, for "solar drying"—at least once in awhile. Many people enjoy the fresh, clean smell of clothes dried in the sun and air. You can, too. In just an hour or two over a weekend you can erect a simple clothes line in your back yard, or in your basement, and give your dryer a rest.

TOOLS AND MATERIALS

Tools required to install an outdoor clothesline are basic: hammer, saw, drill, and shovel. Materials include the 4-×-4 post, preferably pressure-treated; ready-mix cement; scrap lumber for the forms; a broom handle; and a piece of sheet metal (optional).

PREPARING THE HOLE

The clothesline post may be fixed permanently in the ground or set in a socket for removal whenever desired. If the latter is chosen, you will have to construct either a wooden or concrete socket for the posts.

First, dig a hole in the ground 2 feet deep and about 15 to 18 inches square. At·the bottom of the hole, lay a large stone or pour a 2-inch layer of concrete and let it set. The post itself can be made out of 4-×-4 stock. Its length should be about 2 feet more than the desired above-ground height to allow for the portion that will fit into the hole. A form can be made out of four pieces of 1-inch board nailed together so that the outside dimension is that of the post, plus an extra ¹⁄₁₆ inch for clearance. The form should be at least 2 feet 2 inches long. Do not nail the form together too tightly; it might have to be broken out after the concrete has set hard.

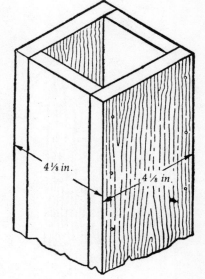

Fig. 25-1. Outside dimensions of form for concrete base.

4⅛ in.

4⅛ in.

Once the hole has been dug and cleared of any loose earth, lay in the stone or concrete and set the form on it, centered in the hole and resting plumb. Secure it in place with four pieces of board tapped down edgewise between the sides of the form and the side of the hole, two near the bottom and two at the top.

Begin shoveling concrete into the hole. Leave the lower board intact, but remove the two above when filling the hole. Shovel in the concrete around the form and tap it down from time to time. Stop about an inch from ground level, so that the top of the form is about 2 or 3 inches above. Don't try to smooth off the surface yet. The concrete will have to be left to cure for a day or more. Cover the hole to prevent soil from falling into it.

CLOTHESLINE POST CONSTRUCTION

Saw off the top of the clothesline post to an inverted V, which provides a surface that will shed water. Saw or sand away the sharp edge at the top. Install a metal runoff cap if desired.

About 8 inches down from the top of the post, bore a hole through the wood large enough to tightly insert a broom handle. At a point 2 inches lower, bore similar hole at right angles to the first, then drive in the broom handles and cut them off. If the handle pegs don't stay snugly in the holes, simply toe-nail a finish nail from the post into the pegs to anchor them.

You can install a pulley arrangement that will allow the line to be raised and lowered for use by shorter people.

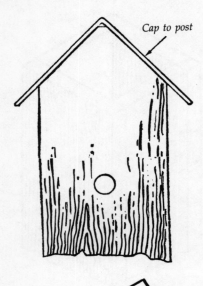

Fig. 25-2. Cap the post to prevent the wood from rotting.

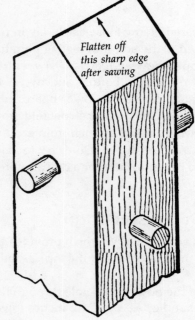

Fig. 25-3. Shaping the top of the clothesline post. Pegs support lines.

FINISHING THE HOLE

Once the concrete in the post hole is set hard, pull out the form and temporarily set the clothes post into the socket. Mix some mortar and lay it on top of the concrete, filling up to the sides of the post, which is left in place as you continue. Make a small box of 1-×-3-inch wood, with the sides measuring 8 inches. Nail only three sides together, leaving the fourth side loose so that the form can be slipped around the post. Place these pieces of wood on top of the cement layer you just applied around the post. See that they are square and level.

Next, fill in the mortar until it is flush with the top of the box. Let the box remain until the concrete sets hard and don't remove the post for several days.

You could install a permanent post, but the disadvantage is that the wood will rot, particularly if it is sunk in concrete. As the wood shrinks away from the concrete, water will get down into the form and remain there. Therefore, it is best to either install a post that can be removed to dry out periodically, or to use good-quality, pressure-treated lumber.

BASEMENT CLOTHESLINE

You can easily string up a clothesline in your basement, provided you have sufficient room. Most important is the depth. Depending on the size of the bedsheets you use, you will want to have the center of the line hang no longer than half the width of the largest sheet. That means a line at least 4 feet off the ground. The alternative is to not hang sheets and larger pieces on the line.

Simply construct two cross bars approximately 3 to 4 feet across and at least an inch thick. Attach eye bolts about 12 inches apart along the length, then attach each of the cross bars at opposite ends of the basement ceiling rafters. You might have to drop a 2-×-4 frame from the rafters/floor joists to allow for clearance of pipes and ducts. Finally, string the clothesline between the eye bolts. Select reinforced clothesline and not simply rope, because the rope will sag with weight of wet wash.

26

Build and Install Bookshelves

With basic tools, you can easily construct a short or tall bookshelf in a weekend. In fact, the time it takes to build two is not much more than it takes for one, because much of the work is in setup.

Tools you will need include a crosscut saw; dado and rabbet blades for your power saw, or special handsaws; hammer; nail set; and clamps.

CUTTING MATERIALS

First, cut out the sides. They will be 1 inch less that the total height. Cut the top and bottom boards to full width. Next, mark the line for the rabbet joint at the end of both top and bottom boards. This will be a little less that ½ inch deep and will extend back from the end to the width of the side boards. Use a tenon saw or tenon blade on a power saw to make the cut. Smooth off the joint, then sand.

Cut and fit all rabbet joints, carefully squaring off the ends of the side boards. Assemble to make sure the components fit, but don't fasten them yet. Cut the two shelves to length, allowing for the depth of the dadoes into which the shelf ends fit. Notch the front corner of the shelf ¾ inch from the front of the bookcase, so that the groove will not be seen from the front.

Now dado the sides for the shelves. Cut to a depth equal to the width of the shelf notch. Slide the shelves into the notches and begin final assembly.

ASSEMBLY

Assemble the top, bottom, and two sides, nailing from the top and bottom into the sides. Use a nail set to recess the finish nails. Next, run a seam of wood glue

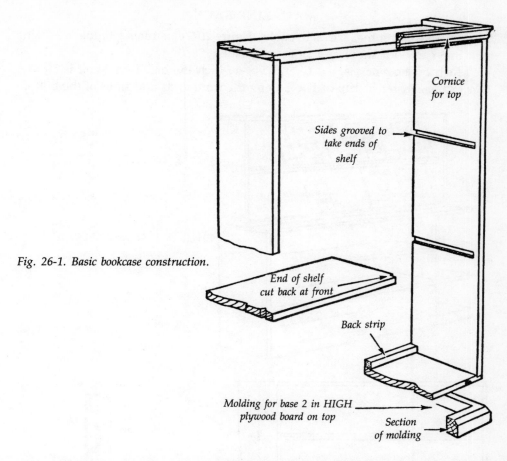

Fig. 26-1. Basic bookcase construction.

Cornice
for top

Sides grooved to
take ends of
shelf

End of shelf
cut back at front

Back strip

Molding for base 2 in HIGH
plywood board on top

Section
of molding

in the shelf notches and insert the shelves into place, tapping them from the back. Any defect in fit will force out the sides, so work carefully, trimming as necessary.

Install a strip of wood at the back edge, then nail a board cut from plywood. This comes flush at front and back. Install the base molding, mitered to fit just under the lowest shelf. Then finish the top of the bookcase with a piece of molding to form a cornice. Cut a sheet of plywood to cover the entire back of the bookcase. Place glue in the joints, install clamps to hold the components in place, and install the back with finish nails.

FINISHING

Finally, sand the unit and stain or paint it to match other furniture in the room. Allow your new bookcase to dry fully before setting it into place.

MAGAZINE RACK

Some people prefer magazines to books. Figure 26-2 illustrates a simple magazine rack that can both show and store magazines.

Much of the stock is 1-×-6- and 1-×-12-inch lumber. Each shelf is 50¼ × 11⅝ inches. Fasten a strip of 1 × 2 along the front ends and sides of the bottom

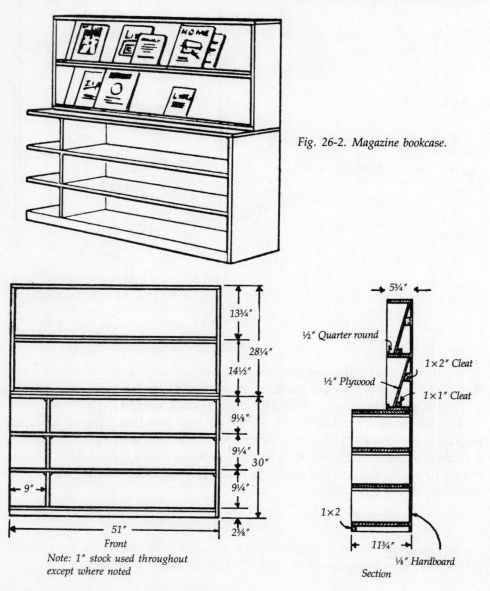

Fig. 26-2. Magazine bookcase.

Note: 1" stock used throughout except where noted

Fig. 26-3. Dimensions for magazine bookcase.

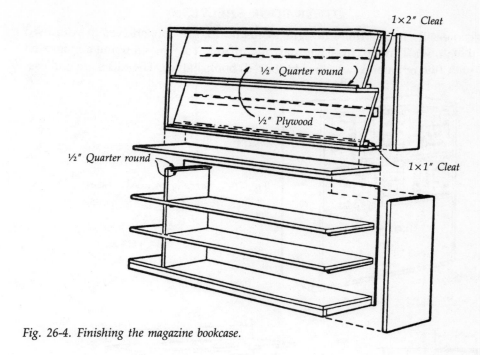

1×2" *Cleat*

½" *Quarter round*

½" *Plywood*

½" *Quarter round*

1×1" *Cleat*

Fig. 26-4. Finishing the magazine bookcase.

shelf to keep it off the floor. Make up the end piece 1 × 12 × 29¼ inches, and the back of ⅛-inch hardboard 30 × 50¼ inches. Assemble these three pieces.

Nine inches in from the end of the lower shelf, install a support for the second shelf. This support should be 8 ½ inches high, cut from 1-×-12 lumber. Put the second shelf in place, use a level to see that it is true, and nail it to the support. Nail it also to the side piece by driving nails through the side, into the end grain of the shelf. Seams where the side piece and support join the shelf can be covered with strips of ½-inch quarter-round molding.

Install other shelves and supports in a similar manner. The second support is the same as the first; the third is reduced in height to 8⅜ inches. The top shelf must be 51 inches instead of 50¼ inches long, because it rests on the side piece.

The magazine rack is made of 1-×-6-inch stock. Top and bottom are 51 inches long; side pieces are 26¾ inches. The back is made of ⅛-inch hardboard 28¼ × 50¼ inches. Exactly 13¾ inches down from the top of the rack, install a shelf 1 × 6 × 49½ inches. The back of the racks is made of ½-inch plywood fastened to 1-×-2- and 1-×-1-inch beveled cleats. To prevent magazines from slipping off, tack ½-inch quarter-round at the edge of each shelf.

OTHER BOOK SHELVES

You can easily modify these designs to customize the bookshelves to your own needs: tall, wide, deep, massive, narrow, mixed. You can combine a magazine rack with two open and two closed (doored) bookshelves. The ideas are endless.

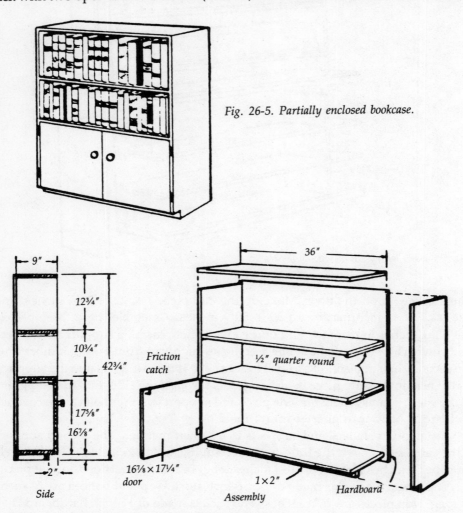

Fig. 26-5. Partially enclosed bookcase.

Fig. 26-6. Construction details for partially enclosed bookcase.

Summer Projects

27

Install a Fire Alarm

Fire is frightening. Most people think about it once in awhile, but are often intimidated by the jumble of wires and attachments they imagine must be involved in a good fire alarm system. And many people just can't afford to have a system professionally installed.

A basic fire alarm system can be easily installed in a weekend. The components can be purchased at consumer electronics shops or large department stores for $100 or less. The components are simple, and most offer detailed installation instructions to make the job easier. Also feel free to contact your local fire department safety officer to get booklets and resources for selecting and installing your fire alarm system.

More information on electricity and wiring is offered in *Effective Lighting For Home and Business* by Dan Ramsey (TAB Book 1658).

The fire alarm is actually a heat detector. It senses the increase in air temperature above a reasonable level (about 135 degrees Fahrenheit), then closes an internal circuit to allow electricity to flow to the sounding device. The sounding device could be tied into your burglar alarm, a separate alarm, or automatically sent by telephone to a nearby fire station or alarm company.

Fire alarms are fairly easy to install. You will need the heat detector units, one for each selected location; the alarm box; wiring; and any required transmission units or telephone. The heat detectors are placed at the center of most rooms: kitchen, bath, laundry, bedrooms, halls, basements, attic. Because heat detectors are not as sensitive to smoke as smoke detectors, they can be installed in kitchens and baths. However, because they are electrical, heat and smoke detectors should not be the only source of fire sensing, because if the fire reaches and trips off a circuit the alarm might not sound. However, many units have small backup batteries.

Wiring is run through walls and can follow electrical conduits to make the job easier. If you are having difficulty pulling a wire through a wall, try a "fish tape," which is available at an electrical supply house.

BATTERY-POWERED SMOKE DETECTORS

Many firefighters consider the battery-powered smoke detectors one of the best inventions of the past decade. They do their job well, and the price is reasonable enough that most homeowners can have two or more. Smoke detectors are often better at sensing a fire than heat detectors, because smoke travels up to the alarm faster than the warmed air. They are usually not as well built as a fully wired fire alarm system with numerous sensors, but many professionals consider them the next best thing—as long as they are maintained and checked periodically.

Installing a battery-powered smoke detector is quite easy. Simply remove the cover, and place the main unit near the center of a room other than the kitchen or bath as directed by the manufacturer. Install the two or more screws, and reinstall the cover. Make sure you use a safe ladder and a helper on the floor to hand you parts. You should also wear eye shields so that plaster or dust doesn't fall into your eyes.

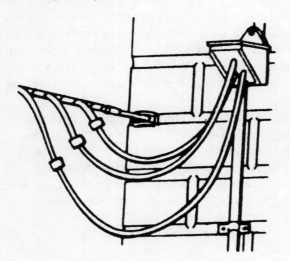

Fig. 27-1. *Make sure that the three-wire electrical system entering your home is in good repair to reduce fire hazard (courtesy General Electric).*

To test the unit, push the test button on all units in your house once a month. Do so on the first of the month to help you remember. Then, every 3 to 6 months, check the batteries in each unit. If in doubt, replace them with quality alkaline batteries.

You might be eligible for lower homeowner's insurance once you've installed a smoke detector or fire alarm. Call your agent to find out.

FIRE EXTINGUISHERS

A fire alarm system isn't the complete answer to fire safety. You should also select and install at least one fire extinguisher, and preferably more, throughout your home. Most fire extinguishers are easy to install; you simply remove the extinguisher from the mounting, and install the mounting to a wall and stud, using long wood screws.

Fire extinguishers are rated by the type of fire they can handle. The Underwriters' Laboratories (UL) classifies fire extinguishers by a letter designation as follows:

A—Ordinary combustibles such as wood, cloth and paper. Useful in garages, workshops and around fireplaces.

B—Flammable chemicals such as gasoline, oil, and grease. Best for garages.

C—Electrical fires. Handy in kitchens and in utility rooms and laundry rooms.

D—Combustible metals. Not normally found in the home.

You can also purchase a combination extinguisher, such as an A-B-C, for your home.

28

Build a Backyard Barbecue

Nearly anyone can build a practical outdoor fireplace. By taking extra time with your weekend project, you can construct an outdoor fireplace that will offer years of enjoyment, and add value to your home.

TOOLS AND MATERIALS

A backyard barbecue can be built of bricks, fieldstone, or poured concrete. Bricks are the most popular because they come in a standard size, are light in weight and easy to work with, and are inepensive. Stones are excellent, provided there is an ample supply nearby—a full barbecue requires a large number of stones. You might also have to split many stones to fit your barbecue. Poured concrete makes a good fireplace, but requires wood forms for construction. It must also be heavily reinforced, especially in colder climates, to reduce weather damage.

Although it is not essential, it is a good idea to line the firebox with firebrick set in a fire clay mortar. Ordinary bricks and mortar will not stand the heat indefinitely, and these materials might save you later repairs.

Other than the masonry, all you need is an 8-×-8-inch flue tile, a metal grill, some sections of pipe, and a piece of heavy angle iron to serve as a front support for the chimney.

Tools depend upon your building materials, but a trowel, shovel, wheelbarrow or cement mixer, masonry hammer (for splitting brick and stones), and a striking tool, should be sufficient.

CONSTRUCTION

Select the site for your outdoor barbecue or fireplace based on prevailing winds. Remember to place the firebox high enough so that the cook won't have to bend or stoop. If there is a natural rock foundation nearby, this would be an excellent place on which to set the barbecue. If there isn't a natural foundation, build up the base to the desired height.

You can follow the plans in this section, or you can easily modify them to fit your own requirements. There is no set rule on what the dimensions of the firebox must be, but 18 inches wide and 16 inches deep is a good size. The walls around it should be at least 8 inches thick, which is the approximate width of two bricks.

When figuring the total area of the fireplace, don't forget the flue tile on the back of the firebox. This will add another 8 inches to the depth. The total depth should be figured at: 16 inches for the firebox, plus 8 inches for the flue, plus 8 inches for the rear wall—giving a total of 32 inches. Calculate the width as 16 inches (two 8-inch walls), plus the 18-inch firebox, equals 34 inches. Thus, the dimensions of the base of this fireplace should be 34 × 32 inches.

Fig. 28-1. Basic outdoor fireplace can easily be constructed in a weekend.

FOUNDATION

In warm climates, it is possible to build the fireplace on a foundation about 4 inches deep; however, in climates that freeze, it must be below the frost line to prevent cracking.

For a concrete fireplace, make the necessary excavation and then build the form for the concrete. The proper mixture of concrete is important. Allow the foundation plenty of time to cure before you begin building the barbecue on it.

Fig. 28-2. *This barbecue will serve your outdoor cooking needs for many years.*

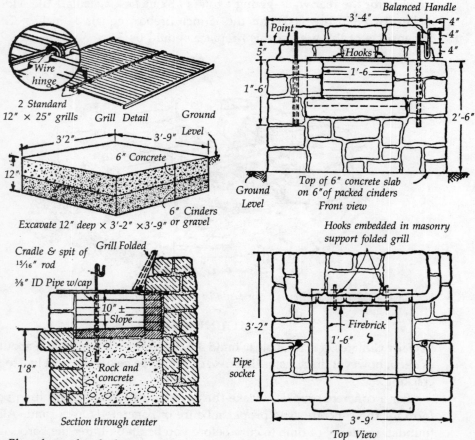

2 Standard
12" × 25" grills   Grill Detail

Wire hinge

Ground Level

6" Concrete

3'2"   3'-9"

12"

Excavate 12" deep × 3'-2" × 3'-9" or gravel

6" Cinders

Balanced Handle

Point

Hooks

3'-4"

4"
4"
4"

5"

1'-6"

1"-6'

2'-6"

Top of 6" concrete slab on 6" of packed cinders
Front view

Ground Level

Cradle & spit of
$^{15}/_{16}$" rod

Grill Folded

⅜" ID Pipe w/cap

10" ±
Slope

Rock and concrete

1'8"

Section through center

Fig. 28-3. *Plans for outdoor barbecue.*

Hooks embedded in masonry support folded grill

Firebrick

Pipe socket

3'-2"

1'-6"

3"-9'

Top View

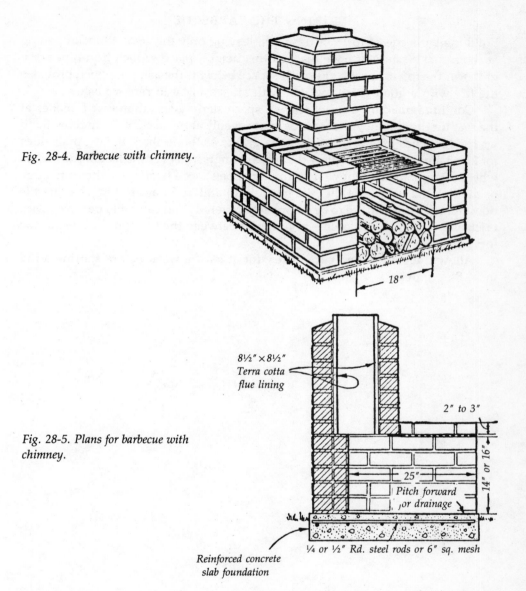

Fig. 28-4. Barbecue with chimney.

Fig. 28-5. Plans for barbecue with chimney.

The mortar for bricks or stone can be made with 1 part cement to 3 parts sand, and 10 percent hydrated lime. Add enough water for a workable mix, but don't make it too watery. Remember, you can always add water, but you can't take it back out.

Wet down bricks and stones before setting them in place to ensure a good bond. Pack each mortar joint tightly.

SETTING THE BARBECUE

Build the barbecue 14 to 16 inches high, leaving only the 16-×-18-inch opening at the front. When you have reached this height, place ½-inch iron pipes or a grill over the top to act as a grate. The space below is the ash pit, which provides the fire with a good draft and you with an easy way to remove ashes.

Continue building up, but leave a space slightly less than 8 × 8 inches at the rear for the chimney. Center this space evenly at the back of the firebox. Build up for 14 inches or more, then set the grill over the firebox. Build up all sides for 2 or 3 more inches, and place the piece of angle iron over the rear of the firebox where it joints the chimney. This iron must be spaced to support the front edge of the flue tile. Place the flue tile in position and build around it. The flue tile does not necessarily have to be completely covered. You can build part way with brick and then make a sloping mortar joint between the tile and the edge of the top bricks.

Allow the barbecue to cure or dry for at least a week before starting a fire in it. Bon appetit.

29

Install a Ceiling Fan

Many years after Humphrey Bogart starred in *Casablanca*, ceiling fans are again in vogue. This time the reason is heating efficiency, to circulate the heat that congregates at the ceiling throughout the room. You can install a quality ceiling fan with just a few hours work, depending on whether or not you require new wiring, and less than $100.

Tools for installing a ceiling fan are simple: a hammer, a screwdriver, wire stripper, and a drill. You'll need a ceiling fan kit, wood screws, 16d nails, wire nuts, and possibly some scrap lumber.

WORKING WITH ELECTRICITY

Electricity is a friend or a foe, depending on how you treat it. If you use it with respect for its power and understand how to control it, you will have no problems. Electricity follows logical laws, and once these are understood you can work with it safely and with confidence. *Effective Lighting for Home and Business* by Dan Ramsey (TAB Book 1658) clearly explains the basics of electricity and how to safely utilize it for many purposes.

The primary rule is: never work on a live circuit. If the old fixture is a light, turn it on and unscrew fuses or switch circuit breakers off until you find the one that controls the fixture. If there is no circuit yet, or if you're not fully sure which fuse or breaker controls the circuit, shut them all off at the main circuit box to be safe.

INSTALLATION

In many cases, you will install an electric ceiling fan where there was previously a lighting fixture. If not, you will first need to install a junction box in the ceiling. A junction box is simply a metal or plastic box attached to a ceiling joist or crossbrace, into which the electrical wires run and from which the fixture hangs. Therefore, you want to make sure the junction box is solidly attached to the house framing, so the weight of the fixture (sometimes 50 pounds or more) will not be unsupported.

Special metal crossbraces can be purchased, and these are inserted into a widened hole in the ceiling to stretch between two ceiling joists. To use them, first mark joist location with an electronic stud finder, and determine whether there is electrical wiring nearby that easily be run to the fixture and controlled from a switch.

In this installation, we will assume that there is already a braced and wired junction box in place, and that no additional support is needed.

The first step in installing your ceiling fan is to remove the original light fixture from the ceiling or otherwise prepare the location. Most fixtures are bolted or screwed into the ceiling and can be disconnected once the cover is removed. Once loose, lower the fixture and disconnect the wires. Make sure they are color-coded; if not, mark them carefully.

The actual wiring is quite simple. First, read over the manufacturer's instructions to determine the color coding of the wiring and recommended installation procedures. In most modern homes, there will be two wires in the circuit and three in the fixture. Connect the black wires together, the white wires together, and then connect the remaining ground (bare or green) wire to the metal junction box or other location suggested by the manufacturer. The ground wire allows a path for electricity, in case there is a short circuit in the other wires.

Finally, check over your wiring, and begin installing the fixture itself. Make sure that all wires can easily be pushed into the junction box without crowding. Also make sure that all hangers and bolts are in place or handy for the installation. Then connect the crossbar or other swivel support, tighten it, and install the fixture cover as directed by the manufacturer.

INSTALLING A FAN LIGHT

If you have purchased one of the popular ceiling fan and light combinations, wiring will be somewhat more complex, depending on the unit. However, the manufacturer's instructions packed with the unit should help you. Basically, you will have two circuits and possibly two ways of controlling them. That is, you might be able to turn on the light without turning on the fan, or vice versa. If this isn't important to you, or you don't want to install a second light switch, simply install all black wires together, all white wires together, and install the ground wires together. Of course, first check the wiring diagram with the unit to make sure that this will work with your unit.

Also consider that a fan light will weigh more than just a fan, so make sure that the junction box in the ceiling can support the weight of the unit before installation. If possible, get above the junction box through an attic or crawl space to visually check and reinforce the box.

30

Build a Deck from a Kit

Many do-it-yourselfers who will add shelving to a closet, replace a bathroom sink, or install a new floor feel uncomfortable building an outdoor deck. Even though deck construction is actually easier than any of these projects, the size is intimidating.

However, major retailers of building materials make the job simpler by offering deck "kits." They include all the materials—lumber, ready-mix cement, fasteners—and the plans you will need to construct normal-sized decks. And any retailer will be happy to modify the plan for a custom deck, if you wish.

In most cases, the cost of a deck is 5 to 10 percent less than the cost of the individual components. This is because of the packaging discount. However, make sure that the packaged price is less than the possible sale price on individual components. If not, find out if a packaged sale price is available. Also negotiate for free delivery.

PLANNING

There are a number of factors that will influence the design, size, and placement of your deck. First is your anticipated use. Will you be using your deck for private sunbathing, large parties, family recreation, outdoor cooking, or some other function? Can you take advantage of gentle breezes or block out prevailing winds by placement or design? Do you want sun or shade or both at different times of the day? Do you need privacy or would you prefer a full view? Should the deck offer entry into a specific room or group of rooms such as the kitchen, dining room, or bedrooms?

Another important consideration is the terrain at the selected deck site. Decks can both compensate for and enhance terrain conditions. You might wish to construct a ground-level deck, elevated deck, or split-level deck.

CONSTRUCTION

There are six components to the typical deck: footings, posts, beams, joists, decking, and railings. These components will all be included in your deck kit, unless you have made modifications.

The first step in assembling your deck kit is to mark off the deck area using string and batter boards. Make sure that it is level and square. The string will help you visualize the size and appearance of the finished deck as well as guide excavation and post installation.

The next step is to prepare the site. With a flat spade, remove sod to a depth of 2 or 3 inches over an area a foot or two larger than the planned deck. Spread a sheet of polyethylene film over the area to keep the weeds from growing up under your deck. You can later cover the film with gravel, bark chips, or clean fill dirt.

Third, install footings. Depending upon your location, footing should be installed at least 24 inches into the ground. Northern climates with deep frosts

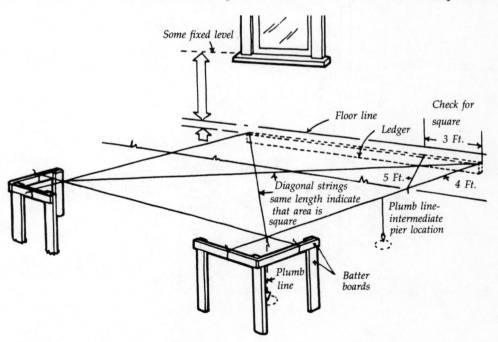

Fig. 30-1. How to measure and lay out your deck (courtesy Georgia-Pacific).

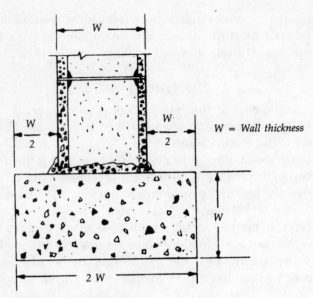

Fig. 30-2. Dimensions for deck footings.

Fig. 30-3. Position and level upright posts (courtesy Koppers).

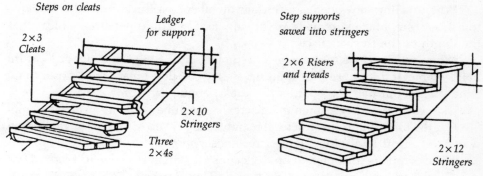

Fig. 30-4. *Two types of stairway stringers* (courtesy Koppers).

should have deeper footings, while rocky areas may only allow an 18-inch footing or even require that the deck be placed on top of the ground. Install the posts within the footings, making sure that they are positioned correctly and are level.

If your kit includes beam straps, install them atop the posts. Then install and secure the beams. Cut the beams to the correct height, which will depend upon whether or not they will support rails.

Fifth, attach the ledger to the house or other building the deck will serve. Make sure it is level. Use lag screws to anchor the ledger to the structure. Expansion shields and lag bolts are required if you are fastening the ledger to a masonry foundation or wall.

The decking is next. How it is installed depends upon the width of the lumber and the design selected. Some decks use 2-×-4 decking placed on end, while others are of horizontal 2-×-6 stock. You can run the pattern all the same direction—horizontally, vertically or diagonally—or alternate patterns.

The rails come next. Most rails are installed by cutting (or installing precut) cross members between posts. Your deck kit might include plans for benches or trellis frames. Follow the directions that come with the kit.

Your deck kit might also include a stairway. If not, have your retailer include plans and materials for one designed for your application. You might require a long unit for an elevated deck, or no stairs at all for a ground-level deck.

DECK CONSTRUCTION TIPS

Following are a few ideas and techniques that will help you install a deck kit or your own custom deck.

Remember to come equipped for safety. Wear gloves when handling wood and safety glasses when cutting wood. If you are cutting pressure-treated wood, you might want to also wear a face mask to protect your throat from chemically treated sawdust.

When nailing, always nail a thinner member to a thicker member: a 2 × 4 to a 4 × 4, etc. Make sure nails are of sufficient length to penetrate at least half the depth of the thicker piece.

When nailing close to the edges of lumber, drill a pilot hole about ¾ of the nail's diameter thick to reduce splitting. Better yet, don't place nails closer to the edge than about half the board's thickness: about 1 inch for a 2 × 4.

Use washers when installing lag screws, machine bolts, and carriage bolts.

Cut the tops of upright structural members to a 30- to 45-degree angle to allow water to run off and minimize moisture absorption.

More complete information on deck construction is available in *Fences, Decks and Other Backyard Projects*—2nd Edition by Dan Ramsey (TAB Book 2778).

31

Install Landscape Lighting

Outdoor lighting serves both functional and aesthetic needs. Step lights, for example, can illuminate stairs that would be dangerous at night. Accent lights show off architecture or plants. Best of all, landscape lighting can easily be installed in a weekend.

TYPES

Incandescent lamps or fixtures add simple and inexpensive sources of light outside the home. Although not as efficient as other types of high-wattage lamps, incandescent lamps are used where lights are turned off and on frequently, or where color retention is important. Outdoor incandescent lamps are available in colors to emphasize decoration, to reduce insect attraction, or to affect vegetation. PAR38 reflector lamps are available in white and colors at 75, 100, and 150 watts. Tungsten-halogen are incandescent lamps with improved light and longer life.

Fluorescent lamps can be used outdoors, provided that a weatherproof fixture is used, the lamps are enclosed in a transparent cover for temperatures below 50 degrees, and special ballasts or fixtures are used at below-freezing temperatures. The efficiency of a fluorescent lamp at indoor temperatures is normally two to three times that of an incandescent. However, in below-freezing temperatures, and without enclosed fixtures, the efficiency is only slightly more than incandescent lamps.

High-intensity discharge (HID) lamps are used for floodlighting larger areas such as roadways, parking lots, and yards. All three types—mercury, metal halide, and high-pressure sodium—require an electric ballast, which is different for each type and wattage of lamp. The fixture shell or housing might be the same for equivalent wattage, but the internal electrical components differ.

Low-voltage outdoor lighting consists of 6-volt or 12-volt lamps, operated from an isolated transformer that converts 120 volts normal power to 12 volts. The lamps are usually 23-watt and 50-watt incandescent. The total number of lamps that can be operated depends on the capacity of the transformer, but it is normally about six 50-watt lamps.

Gaslights illuminate by directly burning gas in an enclosed mantle. The light output of a simple mantle lamp is similar to a 40-watt incandescent lamp. Normally, gaslights operate continuously day and night.

Torches burning kerosene or similar fuels are decorative and portable, for occasional outdoor use on patios and in gardens. For frequent use or unattended operation, camping lanterns offer convenience and safety of operation. Open torches must be kept away from combustible material.

Night-flying insects, with the exception of mosquitoes, are attracted to blue or ultraviolet (blacklight) lamps. Insect traps use ultraviolet lamps, sometimes in combination with chemicals or high-voltage wires, to trap and kill insects. Yellow incandescent lamps provide less light than white lamps, but they also minimize insect attraction. Of the HID lamps, high-pressure sodium attracts the least insects.

Fig. 31-1. Entry area lighting (courtesy General Electric).

INSTALLATION

Electricity and lighting need not be confined indoors. With special devices you can use electricity to light up parts of your home and yard, while minimizing bugs. Remember that, because outdoor wiring is exposed to rain, snow, dirt, varying temperatures, gophers, and other elements, special materials and ~~cedures~~ must be used to ensure that your installation is safe and reliable.

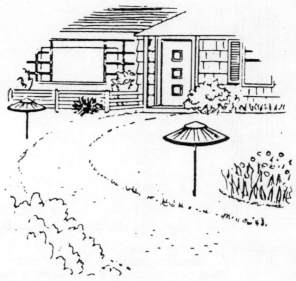

Fig. 31-2. *Path lighting* (courtesy Sylvania).

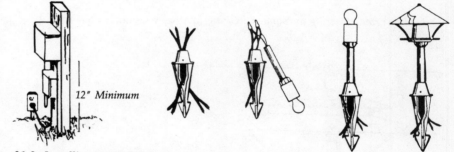

12" Minimum

Fig. 31-3. *Installing outdoor fixtures.*

The National Electrical Code now requires ground-fault protection at the breaker or outlet on any outdoor outlet. To install a light in your yard, first turn your main power panel off. Check to see if you have any outlet or junction box in the basement near the side of the house facing your new installation. If so, you should be able to connect the wiring to this junction box and the indoor circuit, assuming that a 15-amp fuse or breaker can handle the increased load. If there is no wiring handy, you will have to run a circuit from your main panel. Refer to *Effective Lighting For Home and Business* by Dan Ramsey (TAB Book 1658) for specific instructions.

Next, drill a hole the size of your conduit through to the outside, run it underground, and bury it 12 to 18 inches below the surface. If rocks are present,

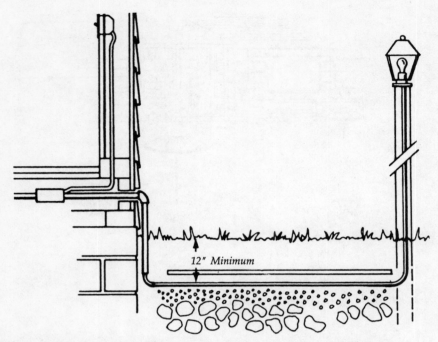

Fig. 31-4. Underground wiring for outdoor lighting (courtesy General Electric).

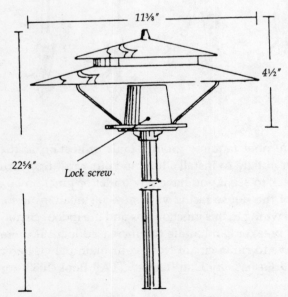

Fig. 31-5. Outdoor lighting designed for wide ground cover (courtesy Loran Inc.).

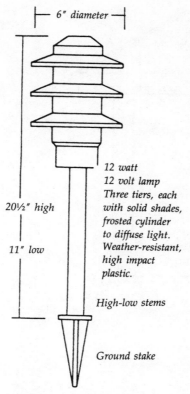

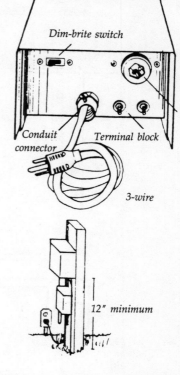

Fig. 31-6. Outdoor tier light (courtesy Loran).

Fig. 31-7. Power supply transformer for outdoor lighting (courtesy Loran).

pour sand around the cable for protection before filling in the trench. A board buried just over the cable will help protect it from shovel damage, should someone start digging nearby.

Run the UF cable to the fixture as indicated in the manufacturer's instructions. Connect white wire to white, black to black, and ground (often green) to ground at the light. Now run the wire from the junction box in the basement through the wall to the switch box inside your home.

Installing low-voltage outdoor accent or garden lighting is even easier. The main differences are the type and wattage of the fixtures and the number of lighting fixtures on a circuit. Make sure that the circuit you choose for low-voltage lighting can accommodate the amperage of fixtures you have selected and plan for the future. First install the transformer, then run wires as directed by the manufacturer, making sure the wires are in locations where they will not be easily damaged.

Have fun in your illuminated outdoors.

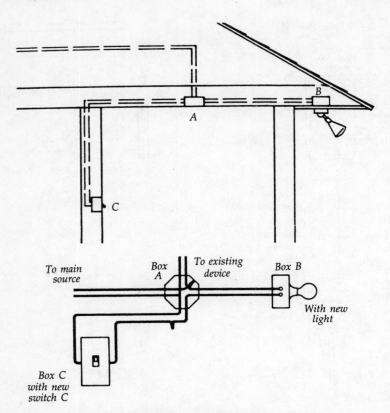

Fig. 31-8. Under-eave installation (courtesy General Electric).

32

Install a Chain Link Fence

Chain link is one of the most efficient fencing materials for new fence construction. It offers maximum visibility, adapts to irregular ground, keeps out most intruders, allows clear air passage, and needs little maintenance for long life.

The major objection to chain link fences is that they don't offer privacy. However, this problem can be overcome through landscaping; with wood, metal, or plastic inserts; and with panels.

Chain link fencing is often less expensive to install and maintain than traditional wood fencing. Many people think that a hiring contractor is required for installation, but you can probably do it yourself. It's easier to install a chain link fence than a comparable wood fence. Many fence supply companies will rent or loan you the tools you need to install your chain link fence.

INSTALLING FENCE POSTS

Tools you'll need include a posthole digger or auger, a fence stretcher, wire grip and stretch bar, cutting pliers, an adjustable end wrench, a tape measure, and a carpenter's level.

Before you start to install your chain link fence on a property line, be sure that the lines are legally established. Unless you have a written agreement to share the fence with a neighbor, place your fence line 2 to 4 inches inside your property line to ensure that the concrete foundation doesn't encroach on another's property. Also, check with local utilities to make sure your fence will not damage underground utility lines.

Determine the location of end, corner, and gate posts—all known as "terminal" posts. Distance between gate posts is determined by adding the actual

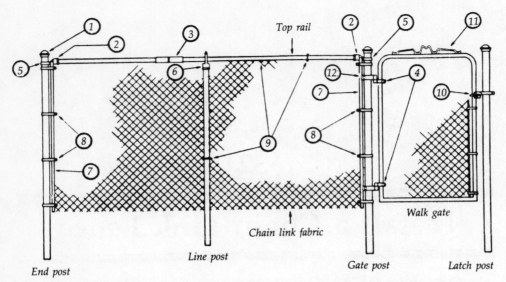

Fig. 32-1. Chain link fence components. Numbers refer to parts on the materials list in Table 32-1.

width of the gate plus an allowance for hinges and latches. Terminal postholes should be 10 inches wide at the top and 12 inches wide at the bottom. Line postholes should be 8 inches wide at the top and 10 inches wide at the bottom. Mark all posts with crayon or chalk for the correct height of fence you are installing. Set terminal posts 2 inches higher and line posts 2 inches lower than the fabric width. Set the terminal posts in cement, using a carpenter's level to ensure that the posts are plumb. Crown all post footings for water drainage by sloping concrete away from the post.

Mark the grade line on all line posts, measuring from the top down. Dig the line postholes and set the line posts. Stretch a mason's line or heavy string line taut 4 inches below terminal post tops, and use it as a guide to align the height of line posts. If it's necessary to adjust the height of any post, simply raise or lower the post before the concrete sets up. Allow the concrete to set up for a day before continuing installation.

After posts are installed and concrete has set, slip the tension and brace bands on to the terminal posts. The tension bands should be spaced 10 to 12 inches apart. Don't spread or distort the bands. All bolt heads for the bands should be on the outside of the fence, and the threaded ends on the inside. Apply all the terminal post caps.

Install the loop caps next. Set them with the top rail hole offset toward the outside of the fence, so the outside face of the top rail is flush through the loop caps. Join the top rail with swaged end where necessary. The end of the top rail fits into the rail end fittings on the terminal post.

Table 32-1. Materials List for Chain Link Fencing.

MATERIALS NEEDED FOR RESIDENTIAL CHAIN LINK FENCE

PIECES	ITEM—DESCRIPTION	QUANTITY TO USE	PRICE EACH
(1)	Fabric (50 feet per roll)	Divide total footage by 50 and round up	
(2)	Top Rail 21' x 1-3/8'' O.D. Swedged	Divide total footage by 21 and round up	
(3)	Line Post 1-5/8'' O.D.	Divide total footage by 10 and round up	
(4)	Loop Caps 1-5/8'' x 1-3/8''	Use 1 per Line Post	
(5)	Terminal Post 2-1/2'' O.D.	—	
(6)	Tension Bar	Use 1 per end or gate post, 2 per corner post	
(7)	Brace Band	Use 1 per Tension Bar	
(8)	Rail Ends 1-3/8''	Use 1 per Tension Bar	
(9)	Tension Band	Use 4 per tension bar or 1' per foot of fence height	
(10)	5/16'' x 1¼'' Carriage Bolts	Use 1 per tension or brace band	
(11)	Post Caps (Acorn Style) 2½''	Use 1 per terminal post	
(12)	Alum Cut Ties	Use 1 per foot of fence — Packaged 100 per bag	
(13)	Walk Gate (3' or 3½' wide)	—	
(14)	Double Drive Gate (10' or 12' wide)	—	
(15)	Male Hinge 2½''	Use 2 per walk gate and 4 per double drive gate	
(16)	3/8 x 3 Carriage Bolts	Used with the male hinge, 1 per hinge	
(17)	Female Hinge 1-3/8''	Use 2 per walk gate and 4 per double drive gate	
(18)	3/8 x 1-3/4 Carriage Bolts	Used with female hinge, 1 per hinge	
(19)	Fork Latch	Needed on walk gates only — 1 per gate	

TOOLS YOU WILL FIND USEFUL IN INSTALLING YOUR FENCE

1. Post Hole Digger
2. Wheelbarrow, shovel and hoe to mix and transport concrete
3. Tape Measure
4. Level
5. String and Stakes or Mason's Line
6. Pliers
7. Fence Stretcher (Block and tackle, ratchet type power pull, etc.
8. 1/2'' x 9/16'' Wrench or Crescent Wrench
9. Hacksaw or Pipe Cutter.

INSTALLING FENCE FABRIC

After assembling the next framework, unroll the fabric on the ground along the fence line, starting at a terminal post. Install the fabric with the smooth edge up, unless it is a security fence which you install with barbs up. Slide the tension bar through the last link in the fabric. Attach this combination to the terminal post using the tension band and bolts provided. If more or less fabric is needed to span the opening, an additional amount can be connected or removed. The fabric should be on the outside face of all posts, with either the knuckled or twisted edge at the top, as desired. Loosely attach it to the top rail with a tie wire.

Stretch the fabric from the terminal post already attached to the opposite terminal post. Insert the tension bar in the end of the fabric and attach the fence stretcher to the bar. A ratchet-type power pull, block and tackle, or similar device may be used. Test for tension as you stretch the fabric. The top should be straight and the fabric should give slightly when pulled. The top of the fabric should be about ½ inch above the top rail for proper height. Remove the excess fabric and install the tension bar to the terminal post with a tension band. Fasten the fabric to the top rail and line posts with tie wires spaced 18 inches apart.

INSTALLING GATES

Gates are installed once the fence posts, fabric, and bars have been placed. Apply male hinges to one of the gate posts, hanging the top hinge upside down to prevent the gate from being lifted off. Loosely apply the female hinges on the gate frame and slip them onto the male hinges. Set the hinges to allow for full

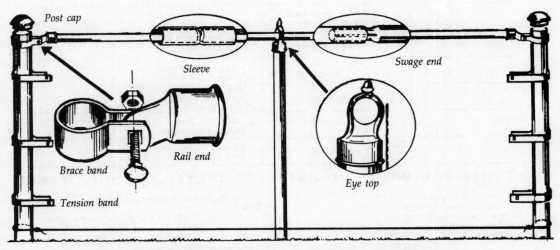

Fig. 32-2. Chain link fence posts, rails, and fittings (courtesy Builders Fence Co. Inc.).

swing of the gate. Align the top of the gate with the top of the fence and securely tighten all hinges. Install the gate latch.

For more detailed instructions on installing chain link, wood, and masonry fences, refer to *The Complete Book of Fences, Decks and Other Backyard Projects*—2nd Edition by Dan Ramsey (TAB Book 2778).

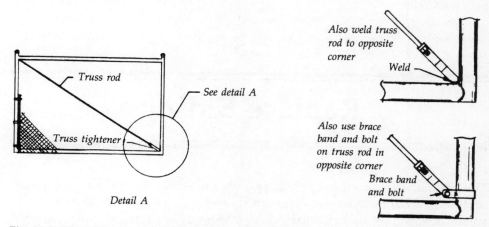

Fig. 32-3. *Typical truss rod and tightener installation* (courtesy International Fence Industry Association).

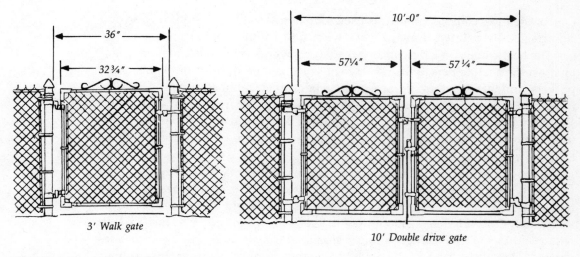

Fig. 32-4. *Single and double gates.*

33

Replace Siding

The selection of siding for your home greatly influences the home's appearance, and also aids in maintenance. You can choose and install siding manufactured from wood, wood-based materials, vinyl, masonry, aluminum, or other nonwood materials. In fact, you can reside your home in a weekend if you have planned the job and purchased materials beforehand.

WOOD SIDING

One of the most common materials used for exterior walls is wood siding. Wood siding is easily painted, easy to work with, and should not warp.

The best woods for siding include cedar, redwood, eastern white pine, sugar pine, western white pine, and cypress. The wood should be free from knots, pitch pockets, and waney edges. Vertical grain or edge grain siding is preferred because it minimizes seasonal movement due to changes in moisture content. The siding should not be too green or wet when installed. Between 10 and 15 percent moisture content is preferable, depending upon the location. Use a water repellent to finish the siding before painting.

Some wood siding patterns are used only horizontally, and others only vertically. Plain bevel siding is available in sizes from $\frac{1}{2} \times 4$ inches to $\frac{1}{2} \times 8$ inches. Usually the finished width of bevel siding is about $\frac{1}{2}$ inch less than the size listed. One side has a smooth planed surface, while the other has a rough resawn surface. Dolly Varden siding is similar to true bevel siding, except it uses shiplap edges, resulting in a constant exposure distance. Regular drop sidings can be obtained in several patterns in 1-×-6- and 1-×-8-inch sizes. It is lower in cost and is often used on garages.

Some fiberboard and hardboard sidings have a backing to provide rigidity and strength, while others are used directly over sheathing. There are also plywood sidings, called panel sidings, available in ⅜-, ½-, and ⅝-inch thicknesses.

Wood shingles and shakes are often used as siding. Wood shingles are available in three standard lengths: 16, 18, and 24 inches. The 16-inch length is the most popular, and has five butt thicknesses per 2 inches when green (designated a 5/2 shingle). They are packed in bundles with 20 courses on each side. Four bundles cover 100 square feet (which is considered one "square") of wall, with an exposure of 5 inches. The most popular shake is split and resawn, with the sawed faced used as the back. The butt thickness of each shake ranges from ¾ to 1½ inches.

NONWOOD SIDING

Over the past two decades, numerous nonwood sidings have begun replacing traditional siding. These include aluminum, vinyl, and masonry veneers. Their advantage over wood siding is that they require less maintenance. In most cases, they are installed in the same way as wood siding, and look much the same.

INSTALLATION

Proper installation of siding requires the correct fasteners. Nails are the most common siding fasteners, and the cheapest insurance. Select corrosive-resistant nails—galvanized, aluminum, stainless steel or similar nails—that will not spot the siding with rust after the first rain. Use finish nails or siding nails. Finish nails are recessed into the siding with a nail set, then putty is applied over them. Siding nails have a slightly larger head and are driven flush with the surface.

Install bevel siding with at least a 1-inch lap. The butt edge of the first course of siding above the window should coincide with the top of the window drip cap. Siding may be installed starting with the bottom course. It is normally blocked out with a starting strip the same thickness as the top of the siding board. Each succeeding course overlaps the upper edge of the lower course. Siding should be nailed to each stud, or on 16- inch centers. Use 7d or 8d nails installed far enough up from the butt to miss the top of the lower siding course. This clearance distance is usually ⅛ inch to allow for slight movement of the siding due to moisture changes.

Avoid butt joints whenever possible. Use the longer sections of siding under windows and other long stretches, and the shorter lengths for areas between windows and doors. If butt joints are necessary, they should be made over a stud and staggered between courses as much as is practical.

Drop siding is installed much the same as lap siding, except for spacing and nailing. The face width is normally 5¼ inches for 1-×-6-inch siding and 7¼ inches for 1-×-8-inch siding.

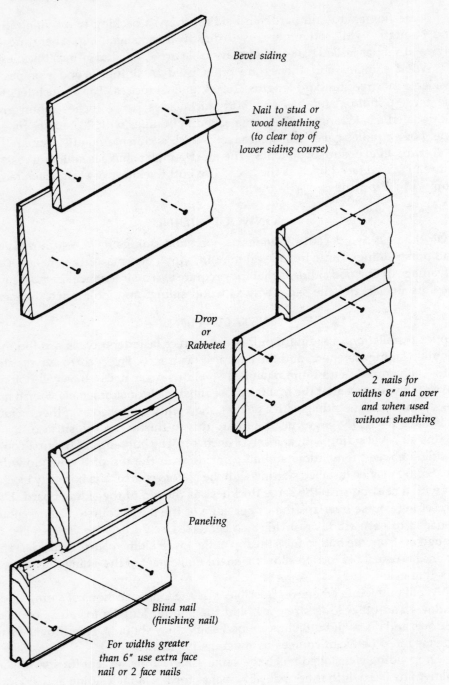

Bevel siding

Nail to stud or
wood sheathing
(to clear top of
lower siding course)

Drop
or
Rabbeted

2 nails for
widths 8" and over
and when used
without sheathing

Paneling

Blind nail
(finishing nail)

For widths greater
than 6" use extra face
nail or 2 face nails

Fig. 33-1. Installing wood siding.

Exterior-grade plywood and related wood products are usually applied vertically. Do nailing over studs. Total effective penetration into wood should be at least 1½ inches at 6-inch intervals around the perimeter, and 12 inches at intermediate members.

Corners can be done as miter cuts, using metal corners or corner boards.

Nonmetal siding is installed in the same manner, except that staples can be used to attach the top edge of the interlocking siding to the wood backing. Follow manufacturer's instructions carefully, because each type and brand has specific installation methods and problems.

FINISHING SIDING

If your new siding requires a finish, first use a water-repellent sealer, then a heavy-duty exterior house paint. Spend a few extra dollars for paint that will withstand the elements, because it will actually save you money by making repainting less frequent. Make sure that your siding is dry first, so that it will absorb your paint for best protection.

34

Install Awnings

Window awnings offer protection from the sun, rain, and other elements, and they also offer a beautiful accent to your home. While permanent metal or plastic manufactured awnings are increasingly popular, there are still many people who prefer canvas awnings. In a weekend, you can easily build and install awnings for a few standard windows.

CANVAS AWNINGS

Besides adding comfort and a pleasant bit of color to your home, you'll find these homemade awnings a considerable saving over the ready-made types. They're easy to put up and take down, and they're especially suited for casement windows that swing outward. The hip gives ample clearance without requiring a frame mounted high over the window, as is usually necessary with conventional casement window awnings.

Fittings can be purchased at a hardware or building supply store. Some ¼ inch galvanized pipe with the end tips hinged in brackets screwed to the wall will do nicely. Sew hems in the fabric as indicated in Fig. 34-1. After inserting the pipes and ½-inch rod in the hems, screw the arms into place.

To keep the fabric taut from side to side, wire the edges to the arms through grommets. Tie sash cord or quality clothesline to each end of the lower pipe, and carry it through the grommets and pulleys. Use a double pulley on the side of the awning where the pull cord hangs down. A cleat, screwed to the window frame or wall, holds the cord.

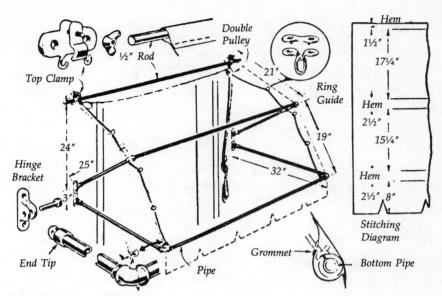

Fig. 34-1. Do-it-yourself awnings.

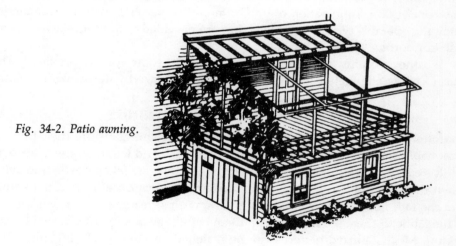

Fig. 34-2. Patio awning.

AWNING WINDOWS

An awning window unit consists of a frame in which one or more operative sashes are installed. They often are made up for a large window wall and consist of three or more units in width and height.

Awning sashes are made to swing outward at the bottom. A similar unit, called the "hopper" sash, is one in which the top of the sash swings inward. Both types provide protection from rain when they are open.

Fig. 34-3. Picnic table awning.

Jambs are usually at least 1 1/16 inches thick, because they are rabbeted, while the sill is at least 1 5/16 inches thick when two or more sashes are used in a complete frame. Each sash may also be provided with an individual frame, so that any combination in width and height can be used. Awning or hopper window units may consist of a combination of one or more fixed sashes, with the remainder being the operable type. Operable sashes are provided with hinges, pivots, and sash supporting arms.

Weatherstripping and storm sashes and screens are usually provided. The storm sash is eliminated when the windows are glazed with insulating glass.

MAINTAINING CANVAS AWNINGS

Too often, neglect rather than weather destroys awnings before their time. A reasonable amount of care will keep awnings fresh and lengthen their lifespan.

It's easy to inspect awnings each year when they are taken down, and again when they are put up. If they are permanent, inspect once in both the spring and the fall. Look them over carefully for any rips, tears, or other weaknesses in the fabric. If there are holes, patch them before the awnings are stored for the season. Most standard patterns can be matched without much difficulty.

To repair a hole, cut a patch an inch or so bigger than the hole and apply it to the outside of the awning with rubber cement, or one of the special glues made for this purpose. A patch applied to the inside of the material is much more likely to be loosened by heavy rain.

Wash awnings before they are stored, not only to remove visible stains and soil, but also to eliminate the residue of acids and chemicals from the air to which they have been exposed. A mild soap and lukewarm water, a stiff brush, and a little energy are all that's required. The awnings, however, must be entirely dried before they are put away in a dry place. Dampness can cause mildew, which can damage the fabric and which is extremely difficult to remove.

The time to examine the pulleys, the cords, and the metal framework is when you remove the awnings. If the framework shows signs of rust, clean and paint it, and oil and grease the pulleys. Replace frayed ropes.

In the spring, a week or so before you plan to hang the awnings, remove them from their storage space and examine them again. If they look drab or faded from last summer's sun, you might want to give them a fresher appearance by painting them before you hang them. Special paints for canvas are available and can be easily applied. The easiest way to work is to hang the awning in place at a low, convenient window. With the awning down, apply the paint with long, even strokes. Finish the whole job at one time. Let the awning hang open until the paint is entirely dry. One coat is usually sufficient, but if a second coat is necessary, do not apply it until the first coat is thoroughly dry.

Here are a few pointers to help you keep your awnings looking their best:

☐ Keep the pulleys oiled and evenly adjusted so that the awnings will not rip when raised or lowered.

☐ Secure the awnings firmly when they are raised, especially in windy weather.

☐ Lower the awnings as soon as it begins to rain so that dirty water will not collect in the folds and stain the material.

☐ After awnings have been soaked by a rain, keep them down until they are thoroughly dry. If they raised while they are still damp, they are likely to become mildewed.

35

Enclose an Open Porch

Two of the greatest sources of heat loss in a house are the front and back door. They are opened many times each day, letting in a blast of icy wind and letting out expensive warm air. Alleviate this problem by building a storm porch around one of the doors, then plan to use any other doors as little as possible.

The storm porch will act more or less as an intermediary between the warm interior of the house and the cold outside. Not only will a well-built storm porch help save energy, but it can be built large enough to provide a place to remove overshoes, and leave umbrellas, thereby reducing the mess in the home.

PLANNING

Size is the first consideration. The porch should be at least large enough so that people entering can close the house door, and have sufficient room to comfortably turn to open the porch door. Better still is a porch large enough to accommodate several people.

The porch can be as decorative as you'd like. If possible, construct the porch out of the same materials used for the house. Your porch will need a roof, which will be either part of your home's's roof or an extension of it. In fact, some open porches were designed so that they could easily be enclosed later by the homeowner.

INSTALLATION

If there is an open porch or large stoop at the front doorway, this can be used as the floor of the porch and a base on which to attach the sides. If there isn't

Fig. 35-1. Small open porch before enclosure.

Fig. 35-2. Small porch after enclosure.

sufficient space, or no porch floor at all, the floor must first be installed. Refer to *The Complete Foundation and Floor Framing Book* by Dan Ramsey (TAB Book 2878) for complete instructions. The new floor should be raised somewhat above the old floor as a transition between the house and the outside. Install insulation underneath the floor frame to reduce heat loss.

Fig. 35-3. Install a banister roof to the porch enclosure.

Fig. 35-4. Screens can enclose a porch.

If the new room is to be enclosed with glass windows, the existing porch railing should be removed and the framework built in its place to support the windows. Cover the lower part of the wall with siding and finish it on the outside to match the exterior of the house. Finish the upper part of the wall by setting selected windows into the newly constructed framework. The interior walls from the windows down can be finished with plywood or composition board, and the space between coverings insulated. Then install the door as described elsewhere in this book.

TEMPORARY PORCH

You can also construct simple temporary walls that will serve as a buffer to the elements in the winter, and stay in the basement the rest of the year. The best method of attaching the sections of temporary porch walls together is with hooks and screw eyes, three sets at each joint. The porch, in turn, is fastened to the side of the house by the same method. Eyelets can easily be installed in wood with a drill; use expansion bolts for concrete and brick walls.

Once the temporary floor is constructed to match the interior floor height, mark the floor for wall location. Then construct a simple frame for each wall, including the door wall. Cut and install plywood panels to fit these frames. Install the door or storm door using manufacturer's instructions. Once all the walls are in place, add the eyelets and hooks, then anchor the walls to the floor using wood screws.

A roof can be added, if not provided by the house, of the same design and materials as the rest of the home. Construct a frame and build rafters that will sit as a unit atop the walls. If costs permit, insulate the roof.

For best efficiency, add weatherstripping between panels, insulate wall interiors, and plan to use dry caulking tape once the unit is installed each year.

Fig. 35-5. Storm windows can enclose a porch.

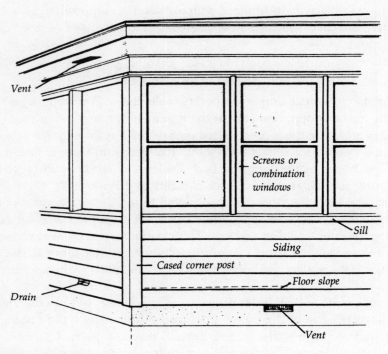

Vent

Screens or
combination
windows

Sill

Siding

Cased corner post

Floor slope

Drain

Vent

Fig. 35-6. Full porch enclosure.

Your enclosed porch is intended to reduce heat loss due to frequent opening and closing of doors. Your new porch, permanent or temporary, can save enough to pay for itself in just a few seasons. And, with careful planning, it can easily be installed in a weekend.

36

Build a Home Repair Center

Home repair can either be drudgery or a rewarding hobby. Proper equipment and adequate work space makes all the difference, and the quality of your work will reflect this. A good job is hard to do with inadequate means. And adequate doesn't have to mean elaborate or expensive. A perfectly satisfactory job can be done with a few carefully chosen tools, well arranged within limited space. Building a home repair center is an excellent weekend project.

A successful repair center—one that fills the needs of the individual—depends upon the type of repairs you expect to make: wood or upholstered furniture repair, large or small appliance repair, electrical repair, plumbing repair, or hobby repair.

PLANNING

The space required for your home repair center can range from a shelf or a table to an entire room. Remember, though, that only fundamental repairs can be made within minimum space. Consider the following as you determine the appropriate amount of space for your repair center: First, it should have enough area to handle the kind of materials you will be using. Work that requires large lengths of lumber can only be done in a fairly large area. Second, the shop should be located where materials can easily be brought in and out if they are large. This is not a problem for small appliance repair, but if you will be servicing larger appliances, you will want an adequate entryway to your center.

Your family will appreciate it if you locate your repair center away from the television or main activity room. You will be happier if you are away from dampness and soot, and have adequate light and ventilation. Finally, but most importantly, your repair center should not be a safety hazard. Make sure you have adequate electrical outlets on a protected circuit. If you paint, make sure it is away from gas pilots and other flames. Play it safe.

You can install your repair center in the basement, attic, a garage, a lean-to, or even in a large closet. Take into consideration whether you are a homeowner or renter, how long you plan to stay, your repair needs, and your budget.

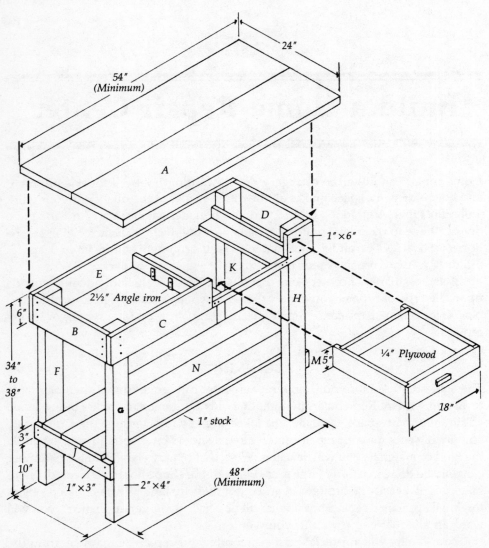

Fig. 36-1. Simple repair bench that can fit into a closet.

TOOLS

The kinds of tools needed will, of course, depend upon the types of repairs you plan to tackle. Here is a list of tools to consider: large and small straight and cross hex screwdrivers, 12-ounce claw hammer, awl, ½-inch wood chisel, 14-inch 10-point handsaw, cutting pliers, long-nosed pliers, jack knife, block plane, assorted paintbrushes, razor blade paint scraper, putty knife, 12-foot metal measuring tape, hatchet, coping saw or hacksaw with blades, 12-inch combination square, 6-inch taper file, nail set, glass cutter, adjustable wrench, 10-inch pipe wrench, 3-inch blade tin snips, test lamp, plunger, electric soldering iron, mason's line, dowel jig, 6-inch try square, 24-inch level, hand or electric drill and bits, C clamps, vise, slip joint pliers, wire nippers, ball-peen hammer.

Specialized tools for special jobs are also useful: upholstering needles, circuit testers, ohmmeter, jigsaw, power saw, bar clamps, oil cans, miter box, etc.

SETTING UP

Once you've determined, and possibly selected, the tools you want in your repair center and the tasks you'll be using it for, it's time to begin laying it out. Consider how much equipment you have to fill it and how much work space you need. If you only expect to work on small appliances, a 3-×-3-foot tabletop will be sufficient. However, to reupholster chairs and sofas you will need at least a 4-×-6-foot space on which to place the furniture, plus working space. The easiest and least expensive way to plan is on paper. Then carry your plans to the actual room or area and begin construction.

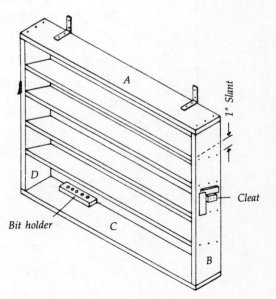

Fig. 36-2. Wall rack for parts and tools.

The most basic elements you will need are storage space, work space, and sufficient utilities: lighting, heat, electrical outlets. Sometimes you can combine all three into one bench or table that offers a work space with storage above and below, and lighting directly above the tabletop.

Sawhorses are very useful in most repair centers, either for holding wood while it is cut or to furnish a base for a second tabletop. In fact, many excellent repair centers are constructed of secondhand cabinets and chests, with two or three sets of sawhorses and a hollow-core door that can serve as a temporary surface.

The illustrations are intended to give you some ideas for planning and constructing your own unique repair center.

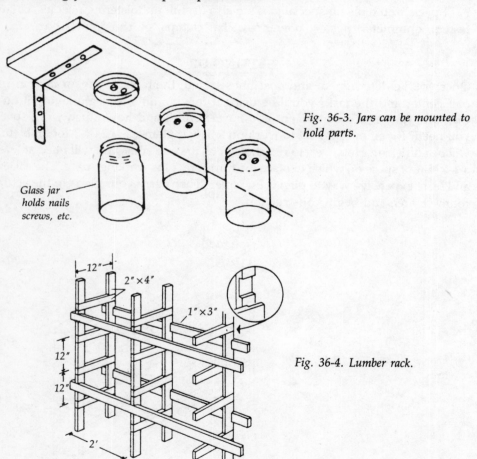

Fig. 36-3. Jars can be mounted to hold parts.

Glass jar holds nails screws, etc.

Fig. 36-4. Lumber rack.

37

Lower a Ceiling

Older homes were constructed with high ceilings that, today, seem inefficient. Because heat rises, much of the air that is warmed is wasted. Heating bills can be lowered by lowering and insulating the ceiling. This can also cover a damaged ceiling or hide exposed joists, plumbing, or electrical wiring. It can easily be done in a weekend.

Suspended or dropped ceilings are simple to install with tools and materials available at most building material retailers. Before you start the job, stop by your retailer and discuss what's involved. Look over the materials so that you are comfortably familiar with how the suspended ceiling system is installed. Pick up any available planning literature, and then go home and do the planning before you purchase.

First, measure out the room where you will install the suspended ceiling. Measure heights as well as widths. Draw the room to scale on a sheet of graph paper.

Suspended ceiling tiles are typically offered in 2-×-2 and 2-×-4-foot sizes. The smaller size work best in smaller rooms such as bathrooms, while the larger size is better for larger and longer rooms. The appropriate size also depends on the size of fixtures you plan on installing in your room. In fact, you might want to select the fixtures before you select the ceiling system, in order to ensure compatibility.

Plan out how you will handle the border of your ceiling. If your room is 11 feet wide, use three 2-×-4-foot panels with two equal 1½-foot border panels.

INSTALLATION

The first step to installing your suspended ceiling is to snap a chalk line along the wall around the perimeter of the room. Measure from the floor or ceiling and use a line level. The line should be at least 4 inches below any pipes or joists, so you are able to install the panels later. Then install the wall track on the chalk line, using nails or screws that are appropriate for the type of wall and relationship to studs.

Next, run strings between the wall tracks, along the path that the main runners and cross runners will later take. Measure to make sure that they are equal distance from parallel walls. Now you can see where the runners need support. Install eyebolt screws in the ceiling or joists directly above the apexes. Loop wire through the eyebolts and twist one end for a secure anchor, allowing the lower end to hang free at least 3 inches below each apex.

You are now ready to install the runners. Install the main runners first, typically lengthwise in the room. Use your string and a level to ensure that the runners are installed at the correct height. Loop the loose end of the suspension wires through a hole in the runner, and make final adjustments before twisting it tight. Install the cross runners next, making sure that each frame formed is square. Once the frame is up, you can paint it if you wish.

Finally, install the panels. Simply tip and push one up through the opening until the entire tile is above the frame, then carefully lower it into place atop the frame lips. you can make minor adjustments to ensure a snug and square fit.

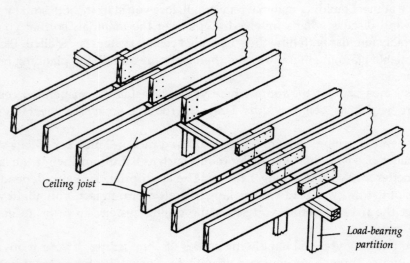

Fig. 37-1. Ceiling joists.

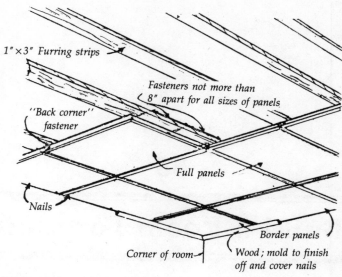

Fig. 37-2. Installing a ceiling.

LIGHTING FIXTURES

An advantage of suspended ceilings is that recessed or indirect lighting can be installed within the panels. Again, you should select your lighting prior to selecting and planning your ceiling system, to ensure compatibility. You should also have planned how you will bring electricity to the fixture and how the light will be controlled. Because your ceiling above may be open or at least unseen, you can more easily find wiring and run it to a location above your intended fixture. Make sure that you won't have interference from ceiling hangers, plumbing, joists, electrical wiring, or other hazards.

It's easier to install your lighting system once the frame is in place, but before installing tiles. Manufacturer's instructions will show you specifically how to attach the fixture to the frame, support it from above, and run wiring. Smaller fixtures will be installed in ceiling tile before being set in place, while larger fixtures will take up the space of a complete panel.

Refer to *Effective Lighting For Home and Business* by Dan Ramsey (TAB Book 1658) for additional information on electricity, wiring, and installing lighting fixtures.

OTHER OPTIONS

You can achieve an effect similar to that of a suspended ceiling by attaching a 1-×-2-inch pine frame and runners to the ceiling or rafter above using nails, wire, or spacer boards. It will take a little more ingenuity, but that's the fun part of doing it yourself.

38

Build a Room Partition

There are many excellent reasons for constructing a new wall within a room or between rooms: Large rooms can be made smaller, closets can be added to closetless rooms, new doorways can be installed. Best of all, you can build a room partition in a weekend.

There are two types of wall partitions. Those that carry structural loads are called bearing or load-bearing walls. Those that merely serve as a means of dividing off the floor area into rooms are called nonbearing or non-load-bearing walls. Bearing walls are more strongly framed than partitions that bear no weight. The homeowner shouldn't alter or remove bearing walls without professional advice, because this can dangerously weaken the entire house structure. Nonbearing walls, on the other hand, can be relatively easily removed or altered by the homeowner, and new partitions put up.

Determining whether a wall is bearing or nonbearing is often difficult without access to the plans of a house. Here are some helpful hints: By looking under your home or in the basement, you can determine the direction of the floor joists. Upper floor and ceiling joists typically run the same direction. Any wall directly above a girder or foundation post is likely to carry the weight of the ceiling joists, and is consequently a bearing wall. Generally, walls running lengthwise through a house are more likely to be bering walls than those constructed across the width. Most houses wherein roof loads are carried by trusses instead of rafters have no bearing partitions in the floor below the attic. Trusses are designed to carry the entire weight of the roof to the outer walls, leaving the space within the house free from the need for support, except for the weight of the floors and partitions themselves.

PARTITION FRAMING

Interior partitions are usually framed of 2-×-4-inch lumber nailed together so that the frame is 4 inches thick. Figure 38-1 illustrates typical wall frame parts, including horizontal sole and top plates and vertical studs. Nonbearing walls usually have single top plates, and bearing walls usually have double top plates. Studs are normally spaced 16 inches on center (o.c.) or 16 inches from the center of one stud to the center of the next. The actual opening is approximately 14 inches. Broader doorways and windows will have double lintels and lap or jack studs.

Materials you will need to install the typical partition include sufficient lengths of 2-×-4-inch lumber, 16d common nails, 8d finish nails, 4d plasterboard or wallboard nails, trim lumber, appropriate size door, jamb, casing hardware, electric cable, and finish materials.

As the first step in installing the room partition, chalk two lines on walls and ceilings about 8 inches apart to locate the partition. Then locate studs and ceiling joists with a stud finder or by tapping. Relocate the partition, if necessary, to bring it in line with existing studs and joists. Measure the space where the partition will go and draw a plan of the new partition based on the measurements.

Next, pry off any baseboards, base molds, shoe molds, cove or ceiling molds, and other trim where the new partition will butt the existing wall. Save the trim.

To begin the actual partition, cut 2-×-4 lumber to the correct lengths for the plates and studs. Lay them out horizontally on the floor as they will later be placed vertically. Using two 16d nails per stud, nail through the plates into the studs.

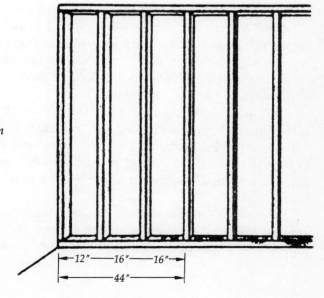

Fig. 38-1. Constructing a partition (courtesy Georgia-Pacific).

Fig. 38-2. Moveable partition (courtesy Georgia-Pacific).

Once constructed, set the partition into place and check for plumb with a carpenter's level. Nail it to the floor, walls, and ceiling. You might need to install wood wedges or shims at various points to ensure a square wall and snug fit.

Before installing the wallboard, locate electricity, shut it off, and run wiring into your new partition as required.

Trim wallboards to size and nail the edge of the first wallboard to the stud at the junction with the adjoining wall, making sure it is plumb. Use 4d wallboard nails sunk just below the wall surface. Remember to cut holes in the wallboard to correspond to electrical and plumbing outlets before installing that section. Also cut and install wallboard above doors and windows, nailing to studs and lintels.

Once all wallboard is in place, the seams must be taped. Some do-it-yourselfers attempt this task themselves; however, inexperienced tapers should have a professional or an experienced friend handle this task. Paint the partition to match the rest of the room or repaint the entire room.

Instructions for installing the door can be found elsewhere in this book. Install trim around the door, and add new baseboards and cove molding to match the old. Finally, pull the electrical wires through and wire fixtures and outlets, and plumb fixtures.

With good planning, your partition can easily be installed and finished in a weekend.

39

Build a Workshop

Building a workshop is a good first project for the home improver. No other project pays better dividends than a well-planned, well-organized workshop. The space used can range from a shelf in a closet to an entire room, but it must be designed for efficiency.

Your home workshop should be convenient, well lighted, well ventilated, and, if possible, separated from the rest of the house for good soundproofing. Also important: Wherever it is located, your workshop should be planned so that it can be expanded and remodeled without undue expense or labor.

LOCATION

Carefully consider the location of your workshop. The basement is the most common and usually the most satisfactory place. In many cases a basement provides sufficient work and storage space, convenient to plumbing and electrical outlets, and adequate heat.

The garage is the next most popular site for workshops, especially in climates where full basements are rare. Many shops today are constructed at the end of a standard garage, because today's shorter cars allow more workspace. The shop can also be installed in one bay of a two-car garage, or along one wall in a wider garage.

The attic is a poor site for a workshop for a number of reasons: the lack of headroom, the fact that all materials have to be hauled up one or more floors, and that typical attics are too warm in the summer and too cool in the winter—especially for projects that require paints or other finishes.

You can also install your workshop in a large walk-in closet, preferably on the main floor; or in a large back porch; or in a small structure installed on a rear deck or backyard.

DESIGNING YOUR WORKSHOP

The design of your custom workshop depends upon its function. A workshop for building furniture and cabinets will require a great deal of space, while one for repairing small electrical appliances can be installed in a closet.

Begin by listing the tools, equipment, and materials that you now have for your shop, as well as those you expect to add within the next few years. Also indicate what you need to operate these tools: electricity, air compressor and lines, space, etc. Next, measure out the space that you have to work with, keeping in mind that you don't have to use it all now. You can save some for future expansion. Transfer this information—space, tools, equipment, utility requirements—onto graph paper.

While you're planning, consider how permanent you want to make your workshop. If you expect to move within a few years, or you are a renter, you should plan workbenches and equipment tables that are not permanently attached.

WORKBENCH CONSTRUCTION

The primary component of any workshop is the workbench. You can find numerous custom plans for workbenches in popular magazines and books. Figures 39-1 through 39-3 give plans for a workbench that can easily be modified for nearly

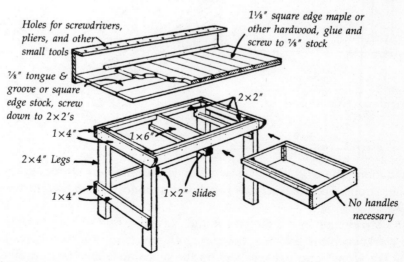

Fig. 39-1. Plans for easy-to-build workbench.

Table 39-1. Materials List for Workbench.

1 piece of 2-×-8-×-12-foot lumber (bench top)
1 piece of 2-×-6-×-12-foot lumber (bench top)
1 piece of 2-×-4-×-12-foot lumber (legs)
1 piece of 2-×-4-×-10-foot lumber (top rails)
1 piece of 2-×-6-×-10-foot lumber (bottom rails)
1 piece of 1-×-12-×-6-foot lumber (tool rack)
16 machine bolts ⅜ × 6 inches
10 lag screws ⅜ × 5 inches
Several pieces of ⅜- or ½-inch dowel

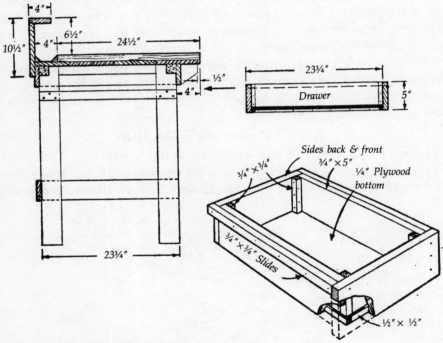

Fig. 39-2. Workbench construction details.

any installation. The workbench shown here is exceptionally strong, yet is ideal for smaller shops. To construct this bench you will need the materials listed on Table 39-1.

Begin construction by building the frame: legs, and top and bottom rails. Then add the workbench top and the tool rack. Remember to drill pilot holes before installing lag screws and use washers on the machine bolt nuts. A drawer can easily be added.

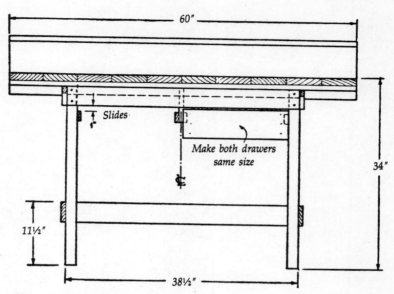

Fig. 39-3. Workbench dimensions.

As you see, this design can easily be modified to match your own needs. You can lengthen the top, replace the tool rack with shelves, add more shelves or drawers underneath, or adjust the height as required. In addition, you can modify this design into an L shaped corner bench or use as the base for a radial arm saw.

Most important, planning and building your own workshop can save you time, and make home improvements easier.

Fall Projects

40

Insulate an Attic

Ordinary building materials offer inadequate protection against extremes of heat and cold. Even the well-built house without adequate weatherproofing is likely to be cold in winter and hot in summer. Insulation materials, however, serve as barriers against temperature change and, if properly used, add greatly to year-round comfort and economy.

Because more than 25 percent of the heat in most houses is lost through the roof, attics are the first place to install insulation.

TYPES OF INSULATION

Blanket and batt insulation is available in strips or rolls that are 1 to 3½ inches thick, and 16 to 24 inches wide. Blankets come in rolls up to 100 feet long; batts are about 4 feet long. Both types can be purchased with a vapor barrier on one side and protective paper on the other. Some manufacturers make their batts and blankets with paper flanges at the sides, for nailing the material to the studs, joints, or rafters. Others provide enough looseness in the paper covering so that the flange can be formed as the insulation is installed.

Loose fill insulation is sold in bags. It can be poured, hand packed, or blown into place, depending on the type. Materials used include rock or glass wool, wood fibers, shredded bark, cork, wood pulp products, vermiculite, and sawdust. Most building material retailers that sell loose filled insulation also rent or loan insulation blowers.

Board insulation comes in ½- and ¾-inch thicknesses, and is made of tiles and panels from a foot square on up in size. The easiest way to install the boards is to nail them directly to the studs or to the old wall, then cover them with paint,

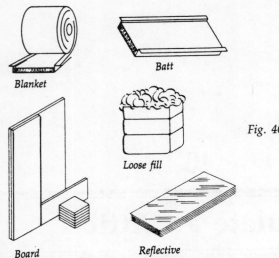

Fig. 40-1. Types of insulation.

paneling, or other finish. Board insulation can be left bare in unfinished antics. In most cases, board insulation has less insulating value per square foot than batts.

Reflective insulation is made of metal foil or sheets, usually aluminum or stainless steel. Its heat-reflecting quality is most valuable in keeping out summer heat, but it is also effective in colder areas, particularly in combination with batt or blanket insulation. Reflective foils and sheets also serve as a vapor barrier.

A safety note: The best insulating materials are fireproof, and act as firestops in the walls. "Flame-proof" materials are not actually fireproof, though they do do retard the spread of fire.

The insulating value of insulation materials are expressed as K-values or heat conductivity. A K is the amount of heat, in BTUs, that will pass in 1 hour through 1 square foot of material 1 inch thick per 1 degree Fahrenheit temperature difference between faces of the material. Simply expressed, K-value represents heat loss; the lower this numerical value, the better the insulating qualities.

Insulation is also rated on its resistance or R-value, which is merely another expression of its insulating value. The R-value is usually expressed as the total resistance of the wall or of a thick insulating blanket or batt, whereas K-value is the rating per inch of thickness. For example, if a K-value of 1 inch of insulation is 0.25, the resistance, or R-value is 1 divided by 0.25 or 4. If there is three inches of this insulation, the total R-value is 3×4, or 12.

INSTALLATION

Place blanket or batt insulation with a vapor barrier between framing members so that the tabs of the barriers lap the edges of the studs as well as the top and bottom plates. For insulation without a barrier, a plastic film vapor barrier such as 4-mil polyethylene is commonly used to envelope the entire area.

Fill insulation is commonly used in ceilings and attic floors. Pour or blow it into place. It's best to use a vapor barrier on the bottom or warm side before placing insulation. Attach a leveling board to the end of broom handle and drag it across the top of rafters for a constant insulation thickness. For thicker ceilings in colder climates, a combination of batt and fill insulation might be installed to increase the R-value. Ceiling insulation 6 or more inches thick greatly reduces heat loss in the winter and also provides summertime protection.

Where attic space is unheated and a stairway is included, install insulation around the stairway as well as in the attic floor. Weatherstrip the door leading to the attic to prevent heat loss.

Ventilation is especially important in attics where insulation has been added. Without ventilation, an attic space can become very hot, holding the heat for many hours. Obviously, more heat will be transmitted through the ceiling when the attic temperature is 150 degrees Fahrenheit than if it is 100 to 120 degrees.

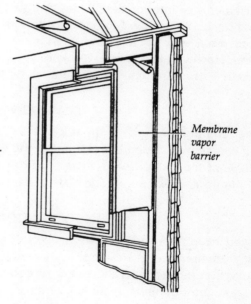

Fig. 40-2. Insulating walls.

Membrane vapor barrier

41

Remodel a Fireplace

Many elements of interior design can change over the years, but the fireplace usually remains the same. Modern furniture, drapes, and decorating schemes therefore often end up in contrast with ornate, old-fashioned mantles and fireplaces. However, in just one weekend, you can easily remodel a fireplace into an attractive structure that compliments your decorative style.

PREPARATION

First, determine how much of the brick, tile, or stone facing you want to leave. This, of course, will depend on the size of the fireplace opening and on the size and shape of the room. Because the brick or tile also serves as insulation, the facing should also extend an adequate distance beyond the opening.

INSTALLATION

Once you have removed the excess decoration, there are several methods of finishing the fireplace. For example, a paneling of broad vertical boards may be set above the fireplace and allowed to extend downward along the sides, with an equal amount of space at the top and each side of the opening. If the brick facing extends outward from the wall, the wood paneling may be finished flush with it. If not, a simple wood molding may be set around the edge of the paneling to finish it off.

Plywood or fireproof wallboard can be applied the same way as the wood paneling. An advantage of these materials is that a single large sheet can usually be cut to fit, thus avoiding seams and joints. If wood paneling is used, it is usually

Fig. 41-1. Remodeled fireplace.

Fig. 41-2. Old-fashioned fireplace with remodeled wall.

simply sanded and varnished. Plywood can be treated in the same way if the grain is sufficiently interesting. If not, it should be painted to match the general decorative scheme of the room.

MANTLE INSTALLATION

In some rooms, a modern mantle is an attractive addition to the fireplace. It should be made of the same material and finished in the same way as the new facing. The mantle may be set at whatever height you desire, but the trend is toward lower and more convenient mantles. You can develop the space above the mantle in a number of ways. The panel is often sufficiently attractive without decoration. If the room seems to demand a center of interest, however, a large picture or mirror will usually achieve the desired effect.

Figure 41-3 illustrates plans for remodeling a fireplace. For this design, you'll need 14 feet of 2 × 7, 7 feet of 1 × 2, 14 feet 4 inches of 1 × 1, 11 feet 4 inches of ¾-inch quarter-round, 25 feet 11 inches of 4-inch V joint boards, and a 1 ¼ × 8 inch by 5 feet 5 ½-inch mantle. You'll also need fasteners as noted in the following instructions. Before you start on the mantle, check the dimensions of the fireplace, because they might vary from those in the illustration.

Remove the old mantle and trim, if any. The 1-×-2 and 2-×-2 stock is used to install nailing bases. Fasten these bases to the fireplace masonry with expansion bolts and to the plaster wall with toggle bolts.

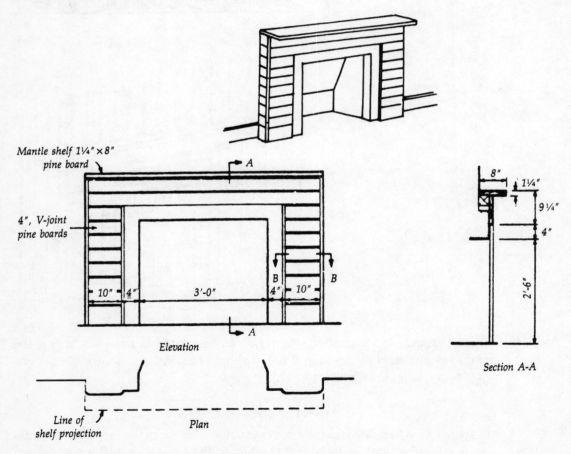

Fig. 41-3. Plans for remodeling fireplace.

Assemble the mantle as a unit and then move it into place and secure to the bases provided around the fireplace. In the case of a pine board mantle shelf, attach it directly to the base over the opening.

The outside corners of the mantle assembly are held together with a strip of 1-×-1 stock running up on the inside of the corner. Run screws through this piece into the 4-inch V joint pine boards. Use ¾-inch quarter-round molding to cover up the outside ends of the boards, as shown. Be sure to leave a 4-inch clearance between the woodwork and the fireplace opening on all three sides. If the woodwork comes any closer to the opening, it could be a fire hazard.

When the mantle has been assembled, place it in position and secure it to the nailing bases with finishing nails. The nailheads should be countersunk and the holes filled with wood filler.

You might have a problem getting a good fit along the top edge between the mantle shelf and the V joint pine boards if the fireplace or floor is slightly out of plumb. Correct this by trimming down the mantle assembly until it fits snugly.

Of course, if your purpose in remodeling is to make the fireplace less conspicuous, you might want to completely eliminate the mantle and not panel the area above the fireplace.

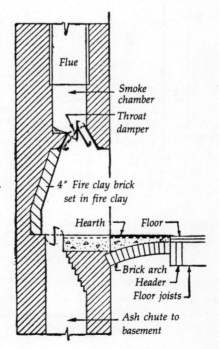

Fig. 41-4. Fireplace components.

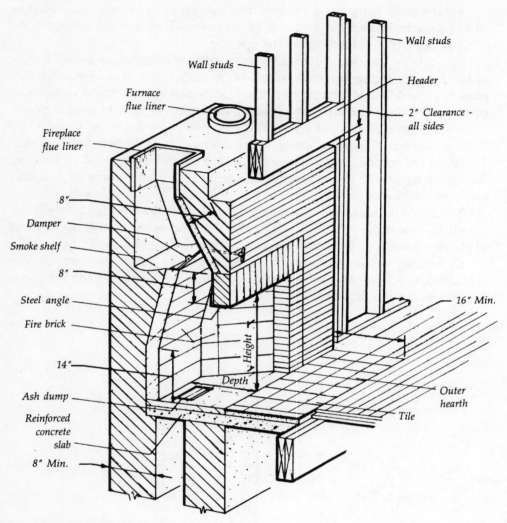

Fig. 41-5. How a fireplace is constructed.

CLEANING THE HEARTH

You can give your hearth tiles new life by washing them thoroughly with soap and warm water, followed with a clear water rinse. Once the tiles are thoroughly dry, apply an even coat of floor wax, which will add luster while resisting dirt and wear.

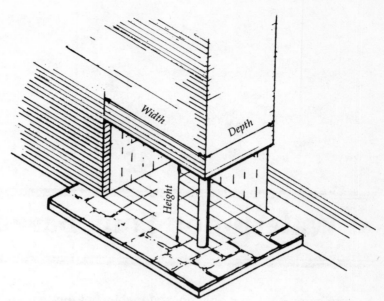

Fig. 41-6. Dual-opening fireplace.

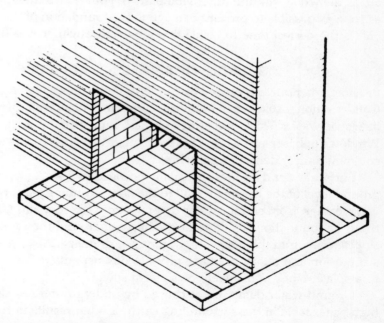

Fig. 41-7. Throughput fireplace.

42

Waterproof Your Basement

A damp basement is not only uncomfortable, but unsafe as well, inviting rot to attack the wood sills and other vital parts of your house framing. Attend to this as soon as possible to prevent damage to the foundation of the house. A weekend is the perfect time to tackle this job—before winter weather begins.

SOURCES OF BASEMENT MOISTURE

Basement dampness is caused by condensation, surface water, or ground water. Condensation results when humid air comes in contact with cold walls and forms beads of water. This ''sweating'' is best remedied by adequate ventilation. Windows in basement walls, fans to circulate air, and louvers set into walls are common anticondensation measures.

Surface water dampness is usually revealed by leak stains running from the ground level of the basement wall to the floor. Running leaks may occur during wet weather, from surface water that falls from the roof and fails to drain away from the foundation. Banking or grading soil around the foundation so that it slopes away from the house might improve drainage. Also, plant the soil to resist erosion and attach drainage pipes to downspouts to carry the water either to a splash block, a dry well, or a storm sewer.

Ground water dampness is caused by underground seepage, springs, or a high water table in the surrounding earth. It often results in running leaks and flooding. The most effective way of insuring basements against this type of dampness is to use membrane waterproofing during construction. However, there are several simpler methods that might correct it after the fact.

INTERIOR WATERPROOFING

One popular basement waterproofing solution is to apply special paints containing waterproofing agents. Another solution is to install an automatic electric sump pump in the basement to eliminate excess water. The third option, plaster waterproofing, is more difficult, but often eliminates the problem so the basement can be used for storage and living space.

First, cut out the rotten concrete in areas affected. Then remove all loose particles and clean the surface. Fill the cracks with an asphalt waterproofing compound. Cut the joint between the floor and the wall into a V groove with a cold chisel, and fill it with asphalt waterproofing compound.

Next, mix a mortar of one part cement and one part sand, plus the proportion of waterproofing agent recommended by the manufacturer. Brush this coat onto the wall. Trowel on a second coat of a mortar of one part cement and two parts sand, building it to a ¾-inch thickness. Finish the patch by steel-troweling the surface.

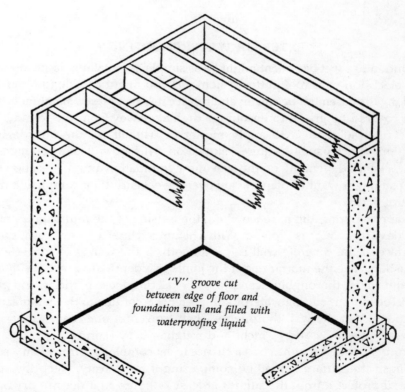

"V" groove cut between edge of floor and foundation wall and filled with waterproofing liquid

Fig. 42-1. Making a watertight seam between basement wall and floor.

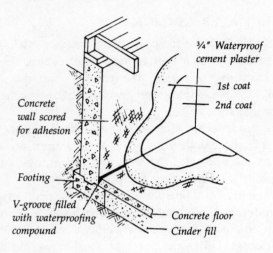

¾" Waterproof
cement plaster

1st coat

2nd coat

Concrete
wall scored
for adhesion

Footing

V-groove filled
with waterproofing
compound

Concrete floor

Cinder fill

Fig. 42-2. Plaster waterproofing.

If you have excessive moisture that you feel will not be stopped by this patch project, consider installing a bleeder pipe or pipes within the patch to draw off leakage to a drain.

EXTERIOR WATERPROOFING

The solution to a wet basement might be as simple as installing downspouts and splash blocks on your roof gutter system. Or you might be able to remove dirt from along the basement perimeter and replace it with a plastic membrane, which is then covered by gravel to encourage drainage away from the foundation.

The final solution is to apply mortar or asphalt on the outside of the foundation, which usually requires excavation. This job will take you more than just a weekend, depending on the size of the foundation and the location of the leaks. You might want to plan the job over a weekend, then complete it during a week of vacation.

To apply mortar, dig a trench along the outside of the foundation until the outer side of the footing is exposed. With a hammer, chisel, or wire brush, roughen the surface of the concrete wall if it is smooth. If the wall is of concrete block construction, rake the mortar out of the joints to a depth of ½ inch. With a wire brush and water, thoroughly clean the wall of all dirt, loose particles, and grease.

Mix the mortar, adding waterproofing agents according to the manufacturer's instructions. Wet the wall thoroughly, then trowel on one coat of mortar to a thickness between ¼ and ½ inch, and roughen it by scoring.

Before the rough coat has had a chance to set completely, trowel on a second coat. Finish the surface smoothly, compacting it for density. Keep the surface damp and protect it from the sun for at least 24 hours so it doesn't dry out too quickly.

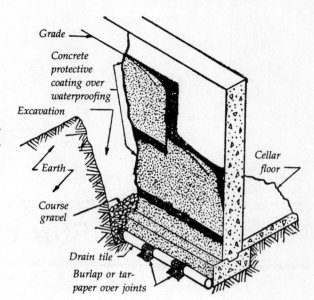

Fig. 42-3. *Waterproofing a basement with drain tile, waterproof paper, asphalt, and cement.*

Next, lay a thin bed of gravel along the trench beside the bottom of the footing. For best drainage, the trench should have a pitch of ⅛ inch per foot. Lay sufficient lengths of 4-inch unglazed, cylindrical clay tile along the trench, extending it about 8 feet past each corner of the basement or connecting it to a dry well. Don't join the tiles, but leave a space of ¼ inch between them. Fold a strip of tar paper over the top of each tile joint to keep out silt. Then cover the drain tile in the trench with stone or coarse gravel. Place tar paper or burlap over the stone fill to keep dirt out of it when the earth excavated earlier is replaced. Finally, fill up the trench with earth, and grade the top so that it slopes away from the house.

You can apply asphalt waterproofing to the outside of the basement foundation instead. To do so, excavate first, apply one coat of waterproofing for soil with good drainage or two for poor drainage, and lay drain tile and rock as above.

For additional information on basement foundations and concrete, refer to *The Complete Foundation and Floor Framing Book* by Dan Ramsey (TAB Book 2878).

43

Install a Storm Door

Fall is an excellent time to consider installing a storm door. Storm doors help reduce heat loss and drafts. Entry doors made of wood and/or metal naturally provide better insulation than glass windows—especially doors with sufficient weatherstripping. Storm doors go even farther: they protect the surface of the entry door from the bleaching action of the sun. So, in addition to saving energy, they also reduce maintenance.

TOOLS AND PLANNING

The tools you'll need for installing a typical storm door include a drill brace and bits, Phillips-head and regular screwdrivers, hacksaw, tape measure, hammer, file, center punch, and level.

Exterior or entry doors are usually 1¾ inches thick. Factory-built hinge doors come in standard widths of 18, 24, 28, 30, 32, 36, and 40 inches, with front doors commonly 36 inches wide. Double-entry doors come in 60-, 64-, and 72-inch widths. Secondary exterior and most interior doors are typically 30 inches wide. Standard door height is 6 feet 8 inches or 80 inches. Nonhinged doors are available in a wider variety of widths and sizes.

To check the door size, first set the storm door in the entry door opening without Z bars. Rest it on the sill and shove it against the side to be hinged (Fig. 43-2). Measure the door clearances at the top (A) and side (B). Clearances for a correct fit are at least ½ inch but not more than 2⅝ inches at the top and at least ⅜ inch but not more than 1⅜ inches at the side.

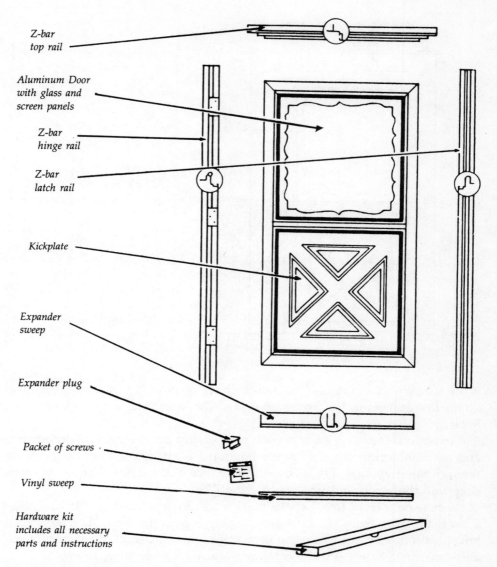

Z-bar
top rail

Aluminum Door
with glass and
screen panels

Z-bar
hinge rail

Z-bar
latch rail

Kickplate

Expander
sweep

Expander plug

Packet of screws

Vinyl sweep

Hardware kit
includes all necessary
parts and instructions

Fig. 43-1. Storm door kit components.

If measured clearances are beyond the limits shown, your door is not the correct size for the opening. Other adjustments and reworks on the door frame will be needed to provide a good fit.

INSTALLATION

To cut the hinge **Z** bar, measure the opening height on the hinge side of the opening. Trim the ends to fit by cutting an equal amount from the top and bottom.

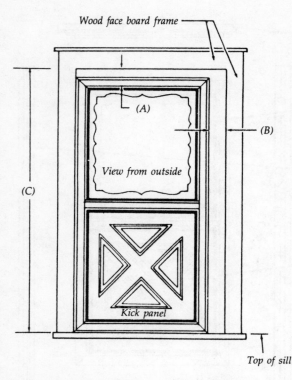

Wood face board frame

(A)

(B)

View from outside

(C)

Kick panel

Top of sill

Fig. 43-2. Storm door kit installation.

If the top and bottom installation holes are cut off, redrill 1 inch from each end on the face and 1½ inches from each end on the inner face, in line with existing holes.

To position the hinge **Z** bar, set it in place against the hinge side of the opening and use the level to ensure that the hinge rail is straight up and down. Mark through the prepunched holes on the inner face of the **Z** bar. Drill holes 1 inch deep into the wood, but don't secure the **Z** bar yet.

Set the door on its side with the hinge edge facing up, and position the hinge **Z** bar so the rail extends ⅛ inch beyond the top edge of the door. The prepunched hinge leaf must be even with the door edge. Carefully mark the center punch and drill hinge holes. Attach each hinge leaf with three short screws.

To secure the storm door in the opening, make sure that all clearance between the top and sides is taken out. Do this using wood strips on the hinge side of the door to shim up the gap, then carefully set the door in the opening. Holding the **Z** bar in position, swing the door open. A block may be used to position the door. Rest the hinge rail on the sill and position it so the prepunched holes are in line with the holes in the wood frame. Secure the inner face with long screws, then drill through the prepunched holes in the front face of the hinge rail and secure it with long screws.

To cut and secure the latch **Z** bar, close the storm door. Carefully measure from the top of the sill to the top of the storm door. Cut the latch **Z** bar rail ⅛ inch longer than this measurement. Measure the gap between the door edge and wood frame. If this gap exceeds ⁵⁄₁₆ inch, a wood strip should be used behind the latch **Z** bar. Mark through the prepunched holes in the inner face of the **Z** bar, drill, and secure with long screws. Drill through the prepunched holes in the front face of the latch rail and secure with long screws.

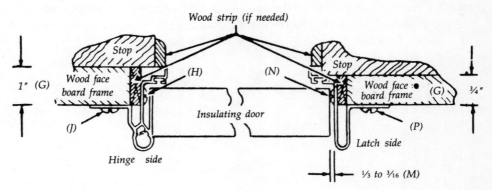

Fig. 43-3. *Door seals.*

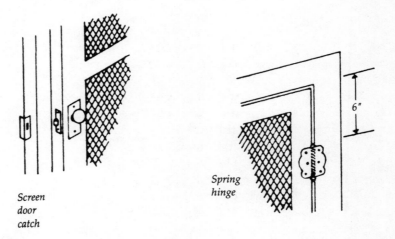

Fig. 43-4. *Wooden storm door hardware.*

INSTALLING TRIM

To install the expander sweep, slide the vinyl into it, crimp the ends, and cut off excess lengths of vinyl. Open the storm door and slip the expander sweep over the base of the door. Close the door and position the sweep to touch all along the sill. When the sweep is adjusted, there will be a gap on the latch side. Measure this gap and with a saw cut a vinyl expander plug to this dimension. Insert the plug in this gap to the latch side of the door only. Drill into the door through holes on both sides of the expander and secure with short screws.

Finally, mount the latch, closure, and chain, following instructions included in the storm door kit.

44

Replace a Complete Window

Until recently, windows were considered merely something to gaze through on rainy days. However, as heating and cooling bills increased, many homeowners became aware that poorly designed, constructed, and placed windows were costing them money.

Windows don't have to be an energy burden. They can become an energy asset, reducing utility bills enough to offset replacement costs. Also important: You can replace a complete window in one weekend.

TYPES OF WINDOWS

The primary types of windows are double-hung, casement, stationary, awning, and horizontal sliding. They are usually constructed of wood, metal, or a combination of the two. Heat loss through metal frames and sash is much greater than through wood.

Insulated glass consists of two or more sheets of spaced glass with hermetically sealed edges (Fig. 44-2). Insulated glass is more resistant to heat loss than singe-thickness glass, and is typically installed without a storm sash. Therefore, insulated glass can actually be cheaper than a single sheet of glass plus storm window.

Wood sashes and window frames are made from clear grade, decay-resistant heartwood or from wood that is treated with a preservative. Species commonly used include ponderosa and other pines, cedar, cypress, redwood, and spruce.

Window glass is known as "sheet glass" and is available in thicknesses ranging from $\frac{2}{32}$ inch to $\frac{1}{8}$ inch. Single-strength is thicker glass weighing about 19 ounces per square foot. Double-strength glass is $\frac{1}{8}$ inch thick and weighs 26 ounces per square foot.

Awning   window   Bow   window   Sliding   patio   door

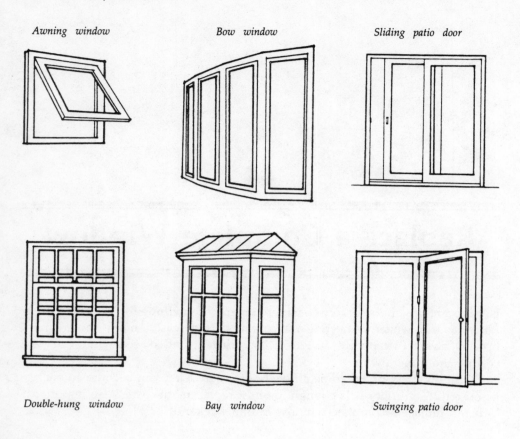

Double-hung   window   Bay   window   Swinging patio door

Casement window   Gliding window

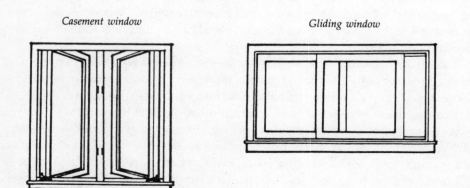

Fig. 44-1. Types of windows.

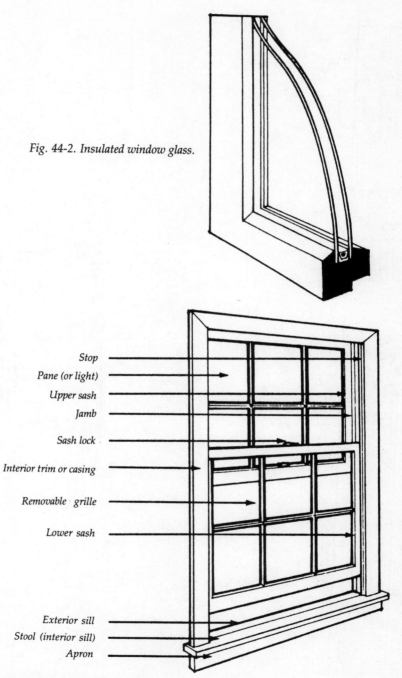

Fig. 44-2. Insulated window glass.

Stop
Pane (or light)
Upper sash
Jamb
Sash lock
Interior trim or casing
Removable grille
Lower sash
Exterior sill
Stool (interior sill)
Apron

Fig. 44-3. Double-hung window components.

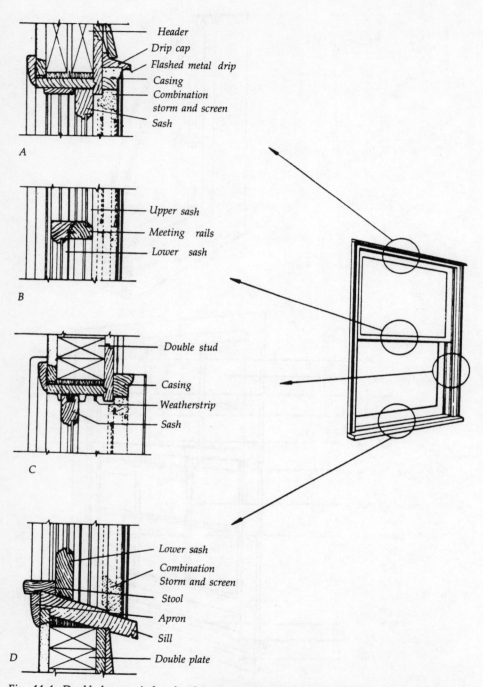

A

- Header
- Drip cap
- Flashed metal drip
- Casing
- Combination storm and screen
- Sash

B

- Upper sash
- Meeting rails
- Lower sash

C

- Double stud
- Casing
- Weatherstrip
- Sash

D

- Lower sash
- Combination Storm and screen
- Stool
- Apron
- Sill
- Double plate

Fig. 44-4. Double-hung window head jamb, meeting rails, side jambs, and sill.

Plate glass is sheet glass ground and polished on both sides for a uniform thickness and little or no distortion. Regular polished plate is used in home construction and is usually ¼ inch thick. Larger windows use heavy polished plate glass, which is ⅜ inch thick or more.

WINDOW SIZES

Windows come in just about every size imaginable. The size of the window is usually the actual size of the opening or sash. Standard sash opening widths for double- and single-hung windows are measured in 4-inch increments, in widths from 20 to 40 inches and heights from 34 to 62 inches. Casement windows have less size variations, but a number of sash groupings. Awning windows range in widths from 18 to 52 inches and heights from 38 to 72 inches.

Horizontal sliding windows and patio doors are offered in widths of 36, 48, 60, and 72 inches (3, 4, 5, and 6 feet), and heights of 24, 34, 48, 56, and 60 inches. Patio doors are usually 80 inches high.

WINDOW REPLACEMENT

The first step, logically, is to remove the old window. Steel casement windows are usually secured by screws into a wood frame and around the window opening. To remove, first locate the screws. They can often be found under the sash itself on venting or operating units. Open the sash and look at the frame for screws. Around picture window units, they might be on the outside of the frame just in front of the glass and covered with putty. Clear away any putty and remove the screws. It might be necessary to use a cold chisel to cut inaccessible or tight screws; they could also be drilled out. Remove the unit from the opening, taking care to prevent injury from breaking glass. For safety, run nylon filament tape over all glass surfaces before attempting to remove the window from its opening.

Aluminum double-hung or sliding windows are usually secured by screws through the exterior flange or through the jamb itself. Remove all screws holding the frame to the wall members and pull the unit out of the opening.

Wooden windows are usually more difficult to remove. Begin by removing the inside stops of the window with a small pry bar. Use a utility knife to break the paint bind between the stops and the wall or trim. Remove all interior trim. If trim will be reused, use a pry bar to gently pull off all members at once, because most trim is nailed together at the miter joint. Remove nails by pulling them through the window with a pair of nippers.

If there is a metal sash run, remove it by pulling the nails with a small pry bar. The lower sash can be removed. Carefully cut any weight ropes or cords, or simply remove them if possible. Pull out the sash carefully to avoid breaking the glass. To remove the upper sash, all parting stop members and metal sash run must first be removed with a small pry bar. Remove the upper sash by pulling out one side at a time. To remove the window frame from the opening, saw it completely through the sill. With this removed, the entire frame can be pried out and easily collapsed.

Once the old window is out, you can modify the wall to the appropriate rough opening size, using instructions offered elsewhere in this book.

45

Weatherstrip Doors and Windows

A drafty house is expensive to heat and uncomfortable to live in. Weatherstripping is essential to eliminate air leakage and reduce heating costs. Here you will learn how to install weatherstripping around doors and windows in one weekend.

TYPES

Experts give two basic recommendations for selecting weatherstrip. First, it should be permanent. Weatherstrip that depends on rubbing action, such as spring metal and bubble thresholds, are not recommended. The second feature to look for in any weatherstrip is adjustability. As exposure to pressure and the natural elements compresses or wears down the weatherstrip, you should be able to make adjustments that freshen its sealing properties.

Weatherstrips are made of metal, rubber, felt, and plastic. Metal weatherstripping is permanent and most efficient, but it doesn't seal as well. The other types must be replaced when they wear out, but usually offer a better seal than metal. The best weatherstrips are constructed of metal and a pliable sealer such as rubber, felt, or plastic.

The five types of weatherstripping are: perimeter or jamb weatherstripping (to go around a door), under-door and window weatherstripping, and thresholds and astragals. The correct one for your job depends upon the application and your experience with tools and materials.

The three commonly used types of perimeter weatherstrip are: interlock, spring and cushion metal, and gasket. The interlock type consists of two metal members—one on the door and one on the opening—that interlock with one another. In cold areas, condensation and freezing can create problems around exterior openings, so in such climates, spring metal weatherstripping is more practical. However, gasket weatherstrip is even better. It consists of an aluminum or bronze retainer strip that holds a vinyl, rubber, or neoprene extrusion; a sponge or felt strip; or plain felt or wool pile.

Gasket weatherstrip is nearly always surface-applied, which means that it doesn't have to be routed into the door or jamb. It is quickly and easily installed, and is usually adjustable.

Under-door weatherstrip is usually used in conjunction with a threshold. There are many types of under-door weatherstrip, including rain drop, spring metal, interlock, door sweep, door shoe, and automatic door button. All are fairly easy to install either on the bottom of the door, on the threshold, or both.

Thresholds fill the necessary gap under a door while attempting to keep out water, snow, dust, dirt, and some noise and light. Thresholds are available in wood, extruded aluminum and brass, cast iron, and steel. They can be used with interlock strips on the door.

An astragal is the weatherstrip installed where double doors meet. Special types of astragals are manufactured for single-acting double doors that only swing in one direction, and for double-acting double doors that swing in both directions.

PLANNING

Most types of weatherstripping and windows can be installed by the inexperienced handyman. The following tools and supplies are needed to do a satisfactory job: hammer, measuring tape, screwdriver, knife or shears, tin snips, handsaw, hacksaw, plane, nails, screws and other fasteners.

Weatherstripping is purchased either by the running foot, or in kit form for specific size barriers. In either case, list the doors and windows you plan to

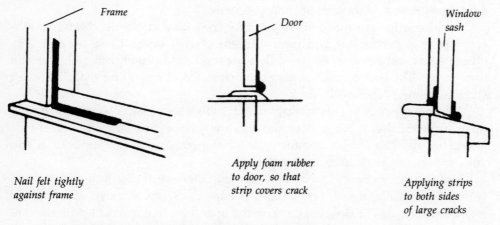

Nail felt tightly
against frame

Apply foam rubber
to door, so that
strip covers crack

Applying strips
to both sides
of large cracks

Fig. 45-1. Common methods of weatherstripping doors and windows.

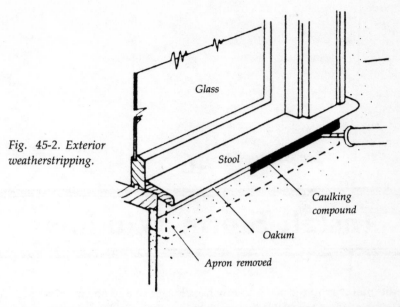

Fig. 45-2. Exterior weatherstripping.

Glass

Stool

Caulking compound

Oakum

Apron removed

weatherstrip, then measure each to find the total length of weatherstripping needed. Measure the total distance around the edges of moving parts. Be sure to allow for waste. If you prefer to buy weatherstripping in a kit, select the one intended for your door or window type and size.

Jalousie windows require a special weatherstripping: a clear vinyl channel that slips over the edge of each set of glass. Finding the correct size and shape can be difficult, but installation is quick and simple.

As for installation of weatherstripping, the manufacturer's instructions are usually complete enough for you to complete the job. You can also ask the clerk at your local building supply how to use the product.

46

Install Storm Windows

The traditional way to reduce window heat loss is to add storm windows. A storm window is simply a second window that attaches to your existing window and creates an insulating airspace between them. Dead airspace, not glazing material or glass, provides the insulation.

The ideal width of the airspace for storm windows is between ⅝ and 3½ inches. A properly installed storm window can reduce heat loss through windows by about 50 percent. If your present windows fit loosely and allow considerable air leakage, your savings could even be greater. A 50-percent reduction in heat loss can mean a considerable savings on your heat bill.

If you want storm windows, you can either have professionals size and install them for you, or you can do the work yourself.

MANUFACTURED STORM WINDOWS

Most commercially built storm windows are made with aluminum frames and glass glazing. Prices vary, but they usually run between $6 and $12 per square foot. Of course, the cost of storm windows are reduced if you install them yourself.

Storm windows function best when they are installed so that they create an airtight seal. The tight seal reduces heat loss caused by air leakage.

Metals conduct heat rapidly. If your present window is framed in metal, make sure that the storm window's metal frame doesn't contact it directly. The two frames should be separated by an airspace or by a plastic or rubber thermal break, to reduce heat loss through the frames.

Aluminum frames can be anodized to prevent corrosion and to offer a color that more closely matches your home's color scheme.

Fig. 46-1. Heat loss through windows.

Fig. 46-2. Poorly fitted storm windows or those that aren't weatherstripped have little insulating value.

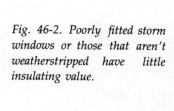

House window
window

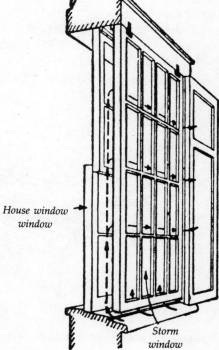

Storm
window

Commercially built storm windows are also available with plastic or wood frames. Both plastic and wood resist heat loss more efficiently than aluminum, but the difference in performance will not show on your heating bills.

Weep holes can help prevent condensation of moisture on storm windows.

DO-IT-YOURSELF STORM WINDOWS

Storm windows can be purchased in kit form, but you can often save money by buying the materials separately. If you make your own storm windows, you can select glazing and framing to fit your windows' individual needs. The various types of glazing materials are equally effective.

Clear vinyl film (8 to 20 mil) and rigid acrylic sheets (80 to 125 mil) are easier to work with than glass.

INSTALLATION

The installation of manufactured storm windows is simple and can be completed by most do-it-yourselfers in a few hours. You'll need a drill brace and drill bit, Phillips-head screwdriver, a caulking gun, and caulk. As you unpack your commercial storm window, remember not to remove the shipping clips on the inserts until they have been completely installed. These clips keep the inserts in position for proper window operation.

To install the storm window against a blind stop, first push the sill extender up. Place the insulating window into the prime window, with both sides of the storm window resting on the blind stop. Push to the top of the opening and drop using wood shims under the extender. Mounting flanges should overlap the blind

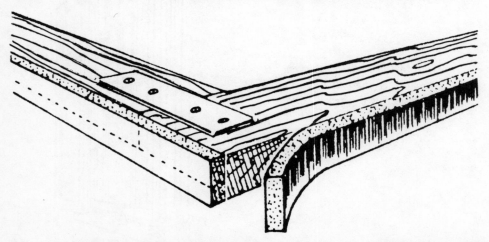

Fig. 46-3. Installing a sealing gasket around the perimeter of the storm window frame will help reduce heat loss.

stop equally at the top and sides. Drill through the prepunched holes in the flanges. Drill through the side flange holes and secure in the same way. Remove shims and adjust the bottom sill extender to fit snugly against the prime windowsill. Remove the shipping clips.

Fig. 46-4. The vinyl glazing can be trimmed after installation.

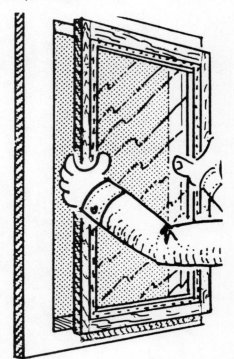

Fig. 46-5. Installing the do-it-yourself storm window.

To install a storm window directly to the prime window casing, place the storm window on the casing with all prepunched mounting flanges resting firmly on the casing face. The storm window must be centered so mounting flanges overlap the casing equally at the sides and the top. Using the bit, drill through the prepunched holes in the mounting flanges. Install screws to secure the top and side mounting flanges. Adjust the bottom sill extender to fit snugly against the prime window sill. Finally, remove the shipping clips.

You can also make and install your own storm windows using clear vinyl film and lath. First, build the frame out of 1-×-2-inch lumber to fit within the window opening. Installing a sealing gasket around the perimeter of the storm window frame will help reduce heat loss. Stretch vinyl film over the frame, then lay the lath around the perimeter and staple into place. Remove excess vinyl film. Finally, place the frame into the primary window opening and secure into place with duplex-head foundation nails, finish nails, wedges, or pressure.

47

Build Built-Ins

Built-ins are functional in that they offer convenient storage space, and they can also be decorative additions to a dining room or kitchen. This weekend, you can select, plan, and construct one built-in or more for your home by following the plans and instructions in this section.

DINING ROOM

For storing china and silver, especially that used for entertaining, it's handy to have a built-in closet or cupboard in a dining room. You can also use the built-in to store electrical appliances and service utensils.

Figure 47-1 illustrates an inexpensive corner cupboard that may be built without tearing out any walls. It may be any depth, but the size shown here will accommodate most articles that the average family uses in serving meals. Built-in cupboards are frequently placed in two adjacent corners of the dining room.

Silverware should be kept in a separate drawer. Three inches is a satisfactory depth for the drawer, unless more than 12 pieces will be stored in a section. If the drawer has a separate section for forks, knives, and spoons, these sections should be at least 2½ inches wide.

Shelves for china need to be at least 12 inches wide. In estimating the distance between shelves, allow 1 inch above stacks of plates, which are handled from the side, and 2 inches above articles such as cups, which are handled from the top.

KITCHEN

Old kitchens often have many doors and windows, it might be impossible or too expensive to move them when remodeling. Use the designs here for cabinets that

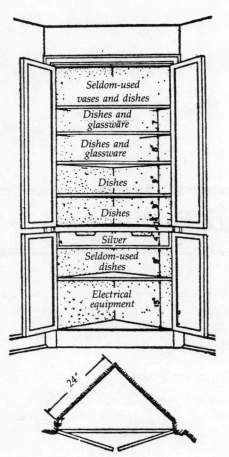

Fig. 47-1. Corner cabinet.

can be used in groups or singly to fit between doors and windows. Each piece is shown in detail with all necessary dimensions, and each is numbered. The numbered pieces are also shown assembled so that individual parts can be easily located.

Materials and tools needed to build the cabinets should be familiar to the do-it-yourselfer. The cabinets as shown are built of plywood and pine shelving. For some of the larger pieces such as ends of cabinets, pine boards are tongued-and-grooved and glued together to form the necessary width. Plywood is used for areas too large to warrant gluing boards together, or where it is needed for stiffening, as in the backs of cabinets. Other materials of sufficient strength may also be used.

Whenever possible, standard dimension lumber—1-×-4-, 1-×-6-, or 1-×-12-inch—has been used full width to avoid ripping and planing. On the

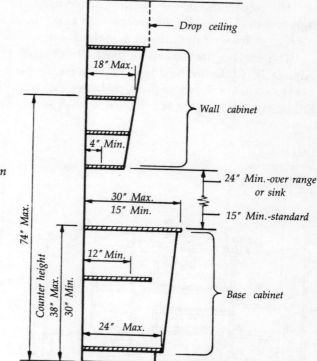

Fig. 47-2. Dimensions for kitchen
cabinets.

drawings, the actual rather than the nominal dimensions are given. A nominal
1-×-4 board, for example, measures about ¾ × 3⅝ inches.

There are notes on design and installation. At 7 feet 4 inches high, the cabinet
will fit in most houses. If a space of less than a foot is left between cabinet top
and ceiling, it is best to close it in with a board or to build a soffit between ceiling
and top of the cabinet. A space of 12 inches or more may be used for additional
cabinets or as dead storage.

No space is wasted between the top of the base cabinets and the top of the
first drawers. The front rim of the sink is kept close to the counter edge.
Nonsupporting partitions and molding are omitted; facing strips are of minimum
width. Dividers are cut without waste of material.

Shelf heights suggest good use of space. These heights provide for storage
of the heaviest and the most often used supplies and dishes, in locations that
are most easily reached.

STORAGE CABINET

Table 47-1 lists lumber and hardware requirements for constructing this storage
cabinet, which is designed to store extra food supplies, canning equipment, and
numerous other articles not frequently used.

The cabinet can be used in the kitchen itself or in an alcove or wide hall. The dimensions—48 × 24 × 88 inches—can easily be changed to fit available space. If space in front of the cabinet is limited, use a double instead of a single door.

The shelves are shown as fixed. If cut from plywood, they can be made adjustable. Racks on the door provide a handy place for small articles. The floor of the cabinet is the room floor, so heavy articles can be slid in and out without lifting. For reaching the top shelves, a small sturdy step box is shown in the plan.

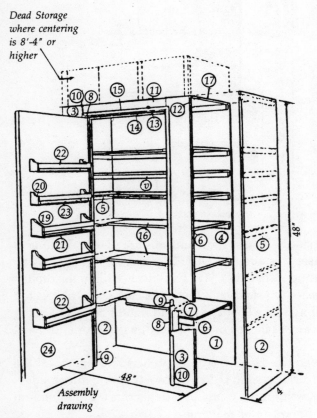

Dead Storage where centering is 8'-4" or higher

Assembly drawing

Fig. 47-3. Storage cabinet design.

Table 47-1. Materials List for Storage Cabinet.

Lumber and hardware	
No. 1 Pine	
1"×12"×12'.....................3	pc.
1"×12"×10'.....................1	pc.
1"×12"×8'......................4	pc.
1"×10"×8'......................2	pc.
1"×6"×16'......................1	pc.
1"×4"×4'.......................1	pc.
1"×3"×10'......................1	pc.
1"×3"×8'.......................1	pc.
1"×2"×12'......................2	pc.
1"×2"×10'......................3	pc.
1"×2"×8'.......................1	pc.
2"×3"×12'......................1	pc.
2"×3"×8'.......................1	pc.
½"×6"×10'......................1	pc.
Plywood ¼"×4'×8'..............1	pc.
Molding	
1" half-round	17 lin. ft.
¾" quarter-round	15 lin. ft.
Door, flush panel, 2'-6"×7'...........1	
Hinges, 3½"× 3½"...............1	pr.
Lock set............................1	
Finishing nails, 4d.................1	lb.
Finishing nails, 6d.................1	lb.
Screws, No. 8-2".................1	doz.
Screws, No. 8-1¼"..............1	gross

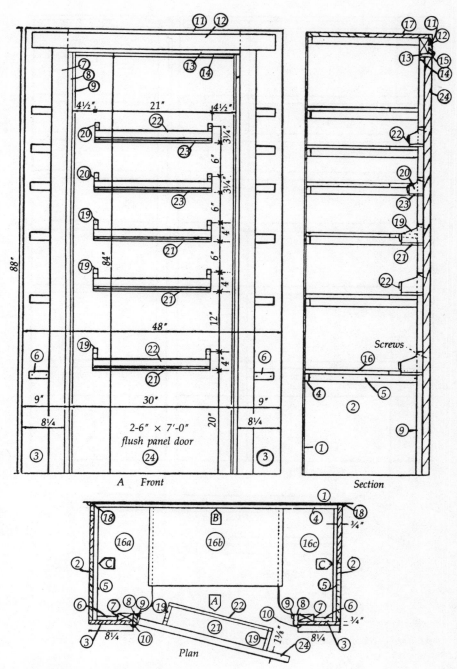

Fig. 47-4. Storage cabinet diagram.

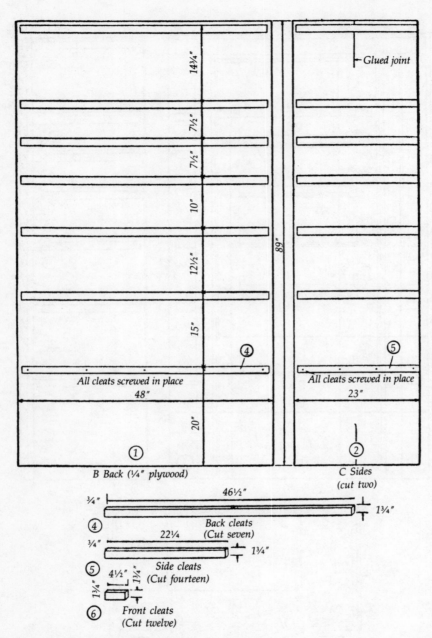

14¾"

7½"

7½"

10"

12½"

15"

89"

Glued joint

④

⑤

All cleats screwed in place
48"

All cleats screwed in place
23"

20"

①

②

B Back (¼" plywood)

C Sides
(cut two)

¾"   46½"   1¾"

④   Back cleats
(Cut seven)

¾"   22¼"   1¾"

⑤   Side cleats
(Cut fourteen)

4½"   1¾"

1¾"

⑥   Front cleats
(Cut twelve)

Fig. 47-5. Storage cabinet assembly instructions.

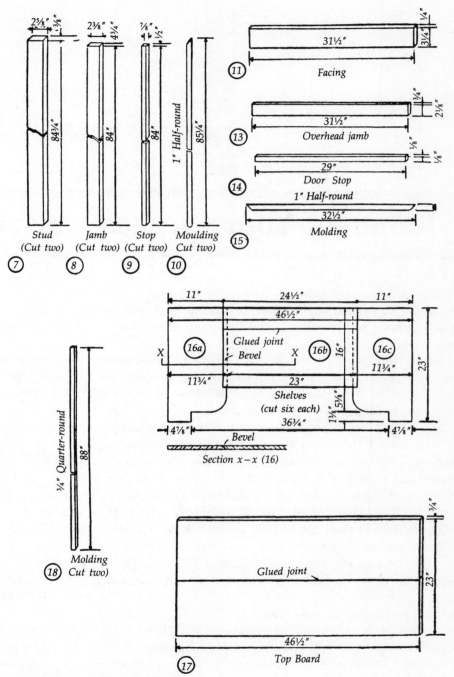

Fig. 47-6. Storage cabinet components.

48

Remodel Your Clothes Closet

A large closet is not always a useful one. All too often the closet is so poorly arranged that much of the space is wasted. However, you can remodel your clothes closet in a weekend, and for many years to come, enjoy the added convenience.

In a large closet particularly, it's possible to rearrange the space so that all of it is utilized efficiently. A closet with double doors can usually be divided into compartments. If the closet is wide, but is fitted with only a single door, you might want to consider installing double doors.

A wide closet is best divided into two sections, with a partition down the center. One of the two sections is used for clothing on hangers. The opposite side can be fitted with drawers and shelves. The drawers should be of various sizes; take care to fit them so that they are as nearly dustproof as possible. A simple method is to cut down an old chest to fit the space. These can be found at secondhand shops or auctions. The top of the chest can be used as stands or shelves. A large shelf can be built across the top to accommodate luggage and infrequently used clothing.

Install a heavy-duty crossbar for hanging clothes. Then install clothing hooks across the back wall for heavy or unpressed clothes. Finally, install a shoe rack across the bottom of this side of the closet. An elevated rack will make shoes easier to find and make cleaning easier.

Don't neglect the inside of the closet doors. Install a full-length mirror inside one door or, if you only have one door, a half mirror across the upper half of the door. The other door or other half can accommodate belts, ties, suspenders, and other small items.

Fig. 48-1. Double closet for maximum storage.

Fig. 48-2. Get maximum use out of a child's single closet.

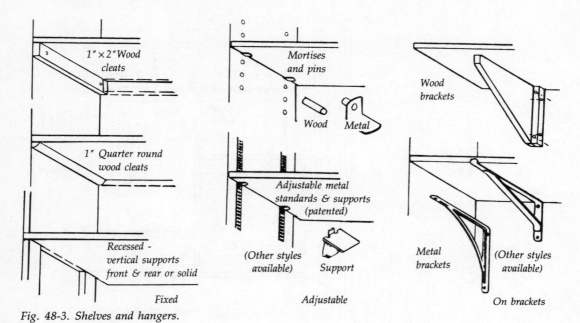

Fig. 48-3. Shelves and hangers.

CEDAR CLOSET

Converting wasted space into a mothproof cedar storage closet can give new life to unused attic space or the corner of a bedroom. The procedure is simple: after you've selected the site, frame it out with 2-×-4 lumber on 16-inch centers. If a part of your new closet uses existing plaster walls or ceiling, locate the stud behind them. Do this using a stud finder or by driving experimental nails into the surfaces. Nail holes cause no problem because they will be covered by the cedar lining.

One of the easiest closet projects is installing tongue-and-groove cedar panels. The sweet smell of aromatic red cedar, though pleasant to humans, repels destructive moths. For this reason, storing clothes—especially woolens—in a cedar closet offers maximum protection. Cedar aroma doesn't kill moths, but it keeps them out of the closet. Out-of-season woolens and furs should be dry-cleaned before storage to kill all moth larvae.

Lining an existing closet with cedar provides year-round moth protection for valuable garments; no home should be without at least one cedar-lined closet. A project of this kind can be completed in a single weekend by the average home do-it-yourselfer, using everyday tools such as hammer, saw, and fasteners.

Red cedar for lining closets comes in strip form. The red cedar boards are ⅜ inch thick, and 1 to 8 feet long. The boards are manufactured in several face widths, from 2 ½ to 4 ½ inches. Cedar lining, available at home centers and lumberyards, comes in bundles or cartons, in random or uniform lengths. Individual pieces are tongued-and-grooved along the edges and ends to simplify construction.

Measure the closet to determine the square footage needed, including the ceiling, floor, and inside of the door. Remove door stops and base moldings, and locate wall studs with an electronic or magnetic stud finder. Snap a chalk line on the wall to indicate the nailing line along each stud.

Apply cedar lining horizontally to the existing wall, beginning at the floor with the groove side down. Then build up, row by row, until the wall is covered. Tap boards down lightly with a hammer to ensure a snug fit before nailing. Only one nail is needed to secure the individual cedar pieces to each stud. Use small finishing nails or wire brads. The interlocking of the cedar's tongue-and-groove

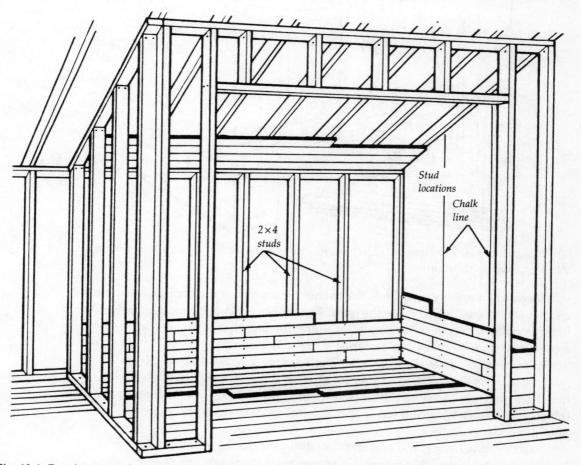

Stud locations

Chalk line

2 × 4 studs

Fig. 48-4. Framing a new closet (courtesy Aromatic Red Cedar Closet Lining Manufacturers Association).

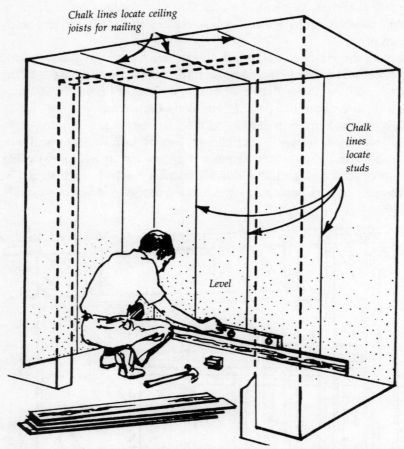

Fig. 48-5. Installing the first horizontal cedar panel (courtesy Aromatic Red Cedar Closet Lining Manufacturers Association).

edges ensures a tight, sturdy fit. If the boards are uneven at the corners, use pine quarter-round molding to cover the gaps. Remember to stain the molding to look like the cedar before installation. After lining the closet, add weatherstripping around the door to make the closet as airtight as possible.

Wipe cedar occasionally with a dry cloth to remove dust that can clog pores. Never use varnish, shellac, or other finish over the cedar, because it will block the cedar oils from reaching the air. If the cedar aroma fades over the years, rub the surface lightly with fine sandpaper or steel wool to open the pores and renew the cedar fragrance.

To determine hanger rod and shelving design, consider what is to be stored. In most storage areas, 4½ feet will be adequate for overcoats and dresses. Most men's suits require only 3½ feet. Hanger rods can be adjusted accordingly.

Fig. 48-6. Installing cedar panels on closet walls (courtesy Aromatic Red Cedar Closet Lining Manufacturers Association).

Fig. 48-7. Installing cedar panels on the closet floor (courtesy Aromatic Red Cedar Closet Lining Manufacturers Association).

49

Modernize Old Sinks

A few hours of weekend work will transform the old-fashioned sink in your kitchen or bathroom into a modern sink and cupboard unit that will give you many more years of service.

Keep in mind that "modernize" doesn't necessarily mean the installation of chrome, stainless steel, and bright-colored plastic. Rather, it is improving the appearance and the functionality of plumbing fixtures and surrounding cabinetry.

PLANNING

The first step in remodeling is to plan the space arrangement of the new unit. The most popular unit is a three-part arrangement, consisting of drawer space on one side of an undersink cupboard, and cupboard space or a drawer-or-cupboard combination on the other side. You might feel that it is most convenient for you to have cupboards on both sides. If so, adapt this plan to meet your individual needs.

You can either build your own cabinets or purchase ready-made cabinets, depending upon how comfortable you are with woodworking projects.

Of course, you might decide that your current cabinets are adequate and that all you need is a new counter top. This, too, can be constructed in place or purchased as a prefabricated unit from your building materials retailer.

If you decide to construct your own cabinetry, build the walls of the undersink cupboard flush to the rim of the sink, extending the front wall at least 2 inches beyond the rim. Make sure that you can sufficiently seal the sink rim to stop water from running under the rim and down the inside of the cabinet. Consider installing full or partial shelves under the sink for cleaning solutions and equipment. You can also add shelves or holders to the inside of the cabinet doors to store cleaning aids.

The cupboard units on either side of the sink should be fitted tightly to the center cabinet. Shelves can easily be installed inside to accommodate the kitchen's supply of pots, pans, and other cooking utensils. You can add a modern touch by installing decorative handles and hinges on your kitchen or bathroom cabinets.

The counter top on each side of the sink and the front ledge should be covered with a hard, water-resistant, easy-to-clean surface such as Formica or ceramic mosaic tile. You should continue this material up the wall behind the sink at least 6 inches.

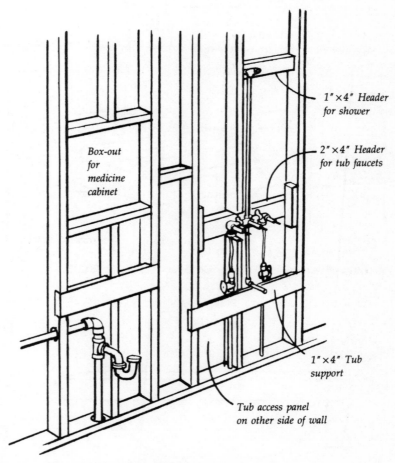

Fig. 49-1. Looking at the plumbing behind a bathroom wall.

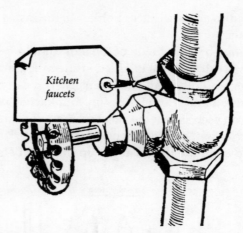

Fig. 49-2. By tagging basement valves you can easily turn off the one going to the room in which you are remodeling.

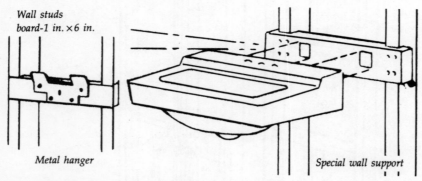

Fig. 49-3. Two ways of mounting sinks (courtesy Sears, Roebuck & Co.).

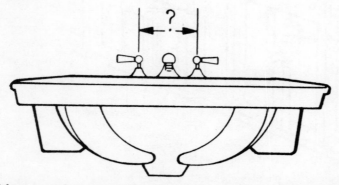

Fig. 49-4. Make sure you have measured the distance between the two handles before replacing the faucet (courtesy Sears, Roebuck & Co.).

50

Build an Attic Study

It's time to start using your attic as more than an area to house a litter of castoff odds and ends. It can be a great place for a hobby room, a study, or a den. Even if it isn't practical to convert the entire attic, it is quite feasible to make part of it into a useful and convenient room.

PLANNING

In most attics, an attractive study may be built around the windows in the gable end. Against the wall under the window, build a desk or table. The simplest way to do this is to construct two separate sections of drawers, spacing to allow sufficient leg room between them. Then build a top across these two sections

Fig. 50-1. Attic study window.

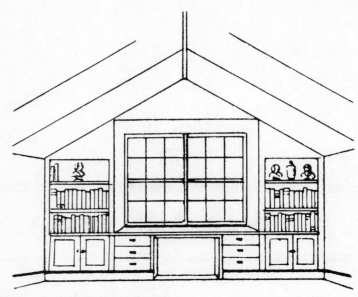

Fig. 50-2. Attic study with desk and shelves.

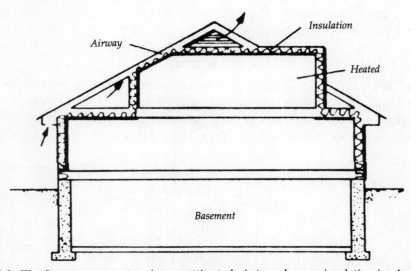

Fig. 50-3. The first step to constructing an attic study is to make sure insulation is adequate.

to serve as a working area. On either side of the desk, build closets, and above these, shelves for books and plants. The whole unit should, of course, be designed to meet your requirements while fitting the available space. Use clear varnish for a natural wood finish, or paint the surfaces in a color to match your decor. Use brighter colors if the attic study doesn't have sufficient lighting.

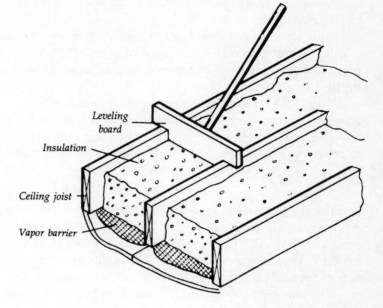

Fig. 50-4. Blown-in ceiling insulation.

Leveling board

Insulation

Ceiling joist

Vapor barrier

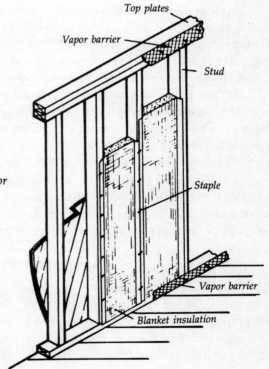

Fig. 50-5. Blanket insulation for attic walls.

Top plates

Vapor barrier

Stud

Staple

Vapor barrier

Blanket insulation

Also provide adequate lighting. Place a lamp on either side of the desk or install indirect lighting.

If the attic has not already been insulated, it is a good idea to give the room additional protection by installing blanket or batt insulation. The insulation will more than pay for itself in reduced heating costs as well as increased comfort in the attic room.

If the floor of the attic is relatively smooth and in good condition, it will probably not be necessary to do more than sand and varnish it, or cover it with a low-cost vinyl flooring. If it is in very bad condition, however, you might wish to cover the entire floor with a plywood subflooring and install tile.

INSTALLING WALLS

Because the purpose of an attic study is to offer a quiet place to read and relax, it is a good idea to install at least a half-wall to separate it from the rest of the attic. This is worth the extra effort. Using drywall you can build such a partition yourself. There are many types of rigid wallboards that can be installed directly to framing studs and that require little further treatment. The most common types of wallboards are plasterboard, plywood, and wood or simulated wood paneling. They are typically available in 4-×-8-foot or larger panels.

The framework of the wall to which the panels are attached should be built of 2-×-4-inch studs, set about 16 inches apart and firmly anchored at the top and bottom on 2-×-4 plates. If the wall is to reach only part way to the ceiling, the top plate to which the upper ends of the studs are fastened should be a double 2-×-4 firmly secured at both ends to make the wall rigid.

Nail the paneling directly to the studs with special large-head nails. Some boards have tongue-and-grooved edges for better panel-to-panel jointing. Others have only one edge grooved so that when two edges abut, a groove is formed into which cement and tape can be fitted to make a concealed joint. Special edge and corner molding is available for finishing the tops of panels and the corners.

The decoration of the room is a matter of individual taste. The new room can be furnished in natural wood, or it can be papered or painted in an attractive color scheme. The attic room, far from the main part of the home, is a particularly good place to experiment with new or original ideas.

LIVING QUARTERS

The attic study can also double as a guest room by simply adding a bunk bed and storage along one wall. For example, divide the wall space along one side into three parts. The center part should be long enough to accommodate a bunk or single bed, and the end spaces large enough for built-in shelves and closets. Place partitions the width of the bunk at either end of the bunk to serve as the end walls for the closet and shelf arrangement. These partitions can be made of plain boards or of the materials used in paneling. Obviously, these units may be varied to suit the space available. If you have sufficient room, one large unit with a closet-and-drawer combination in the base and a smaller unit of drawers will provide convenience. If space is limited, make a single unit at one end.

You might not need to buy a special bunk for the attic room. An unused box spring and mattress from a single bed is ideal. You need only build a low frame beneath to serve as a support, putting in underbunk drawers if additional storage space is desirable. In other cases, a small daybed or even the upper half of a double deck bunk bed will serve your needs well.

51

Furnish a Playroom

PLAY CORNER

A built-in play corner in the children's room, or in a separate playroom, is not only an attractive addition to the room, but also a convenience for parents. A perfectly adequate small play corner or area can be made easily and inexpensively over just one weekend.

One of the simplest and most useful types of built-ins is a plain bench set flush against one wall, or better still, along the two walls in a corner of the room. The bench should be built high enough for the child to sit on it comfortably. It will probably also be used as a table, and it will keep the toys off the floor and greatly reduce the clutter.

The usefulness of this table-bench combination can be further increased by adding a shelf. Do this by making the back of the bench wider and attaching a high raised shelf built flush to the wall above the bench. The shelf may be a simple board set on posts above the bench, or a more elaborate boxed-in shelf that will prevent small toys from becoming lost or mislaid. Either way it provides additional space upon which to put playthings when not in use.

The idea can be carried still further, if there is enough room, by building an oblong table for use in front of the bench. Not only is this table useful for sedentary play and eating, but it will also serve as another bench or a "boat." If the shelf arrangement has been built into a corner of the room it might prove more useful and attractive to build a square table to set neatly into the bench corner. You might also want to build a low sitting bench that can be moved about, placed at the table or the wall bench, stacked on the table to make an elevated vantage point, or pushed back under the table when not in use. You can even enclose the wall bench to make a storage cupboard for the hundreds of possessions that a child

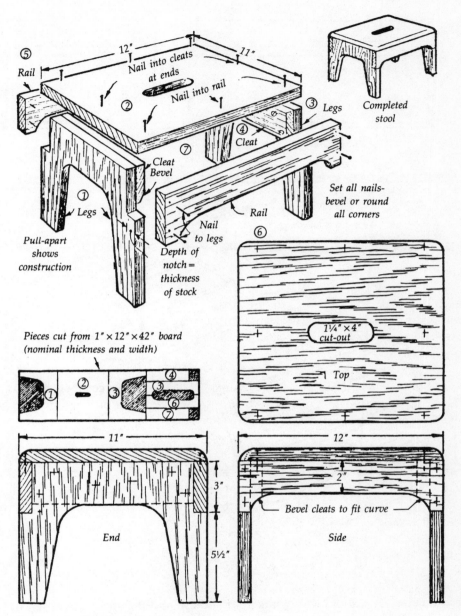

⑤ Rail — 12" — Nail into cleats at ends — 11"
② Nail into rail
③ Legs
④ Cleat
⑦
Cleat Bevel
① Legs

Pull-apart shows construction

Depth of notch = thickness of stock

Nail to legs

Rail

Completed stool

Set all nails-bevel or round all corners

⑥

Pieces cut from 1" × 12" × 42" board (nominal thickness and width)

① ② ③ ④ ③ ⑥ ⑦

1¼" × 4" cut-out

Top

11"

3"

5½"

End

12"

2"

Bevel cleats to fit curve

Side

Fig. 51-1. Utility stool construction plans.

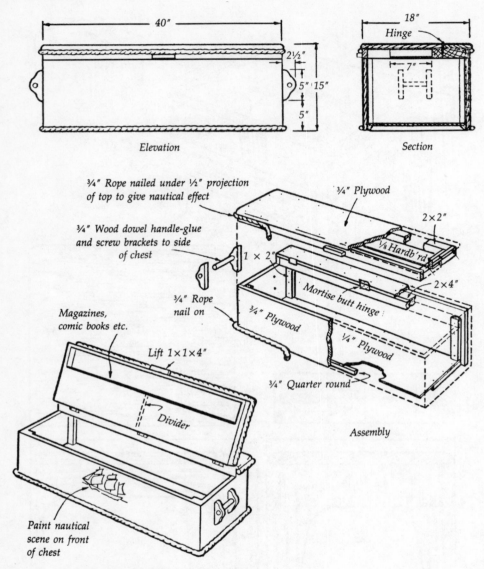

40"

2½"

5" 15"

5"

Elevation

18"

Hinge

7"

Section

¾" Rope nailed under ½" projection
of top to give nautical effect

¾" Plywood

2 × 2"

¾" Wood dowel handle-glue
and screw brackets to side
of chest

1 × 2"

⅛ Hardb'rd

2 × 4"

Mortise butt hinge

Magazines,
comic books etc.

¾" Rope
nail on

¾" Plywood

¼" Plywood

Lift 1×1×4"

¾" Quarter round

Divider

Assembly

Paint nautical
scene on front
of chest

Fig. 51-2. Toy chest construction plans.

accumulates. The door can be hinged or sliding, and the space inside left open
for general storage or fitted with shelves for the orderly arrangement of small
articles.

For maximum durability, a good grade of lumber is ordinarily the best material to use for the unit. It should be free of splinters and carefully put together
so that there will be no protruding nails to cause injury or tear clothing.

**Table 51-1.
Materials List for Toy Chest.**

1 piece	¾" plywood 18"×40"
1 piece	¾" plywood 14¼"×40"
2 pieces	¾" plywood 14¼"×18"
1 piece	¾" plywood 13"×40"
1 piece	¼" plywood 16½"×38½"
1 piece	2"×4"×38½"
1 piece	2"×2"×38½"
1 piece	1"×2"×38½"
4 pieces	1"×2"×12"
4 pieces	1"×2"×11¼"
1 piece	1"×1"×4"
2 pieces	¾"quarter round 38½"
2 pieces	¾"quarter round 16½"
3 butt hinges	

Fig. 51-3. The finished playroom.

Decoration of the children's corner poses no problems. It can be painted to match the walls of the room if you prefer to make it inconspicuous, or it can be painted in a bright and cheerful color to please the child and add an attractive contrast to the room. Wallpaper is another option.

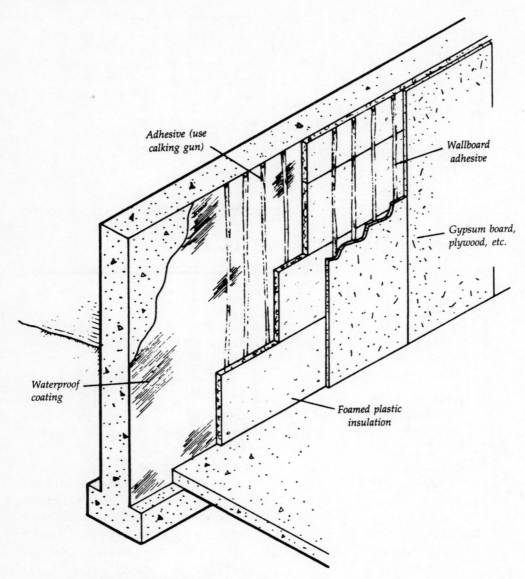

Fig. 51-4. Insulating a basement wall.

52

Build Bunk Beds

The double-tiered bunk bed has always been a popular project for do-it-yourselfers. It offers a practical, yet easy-to-construct piece of furniture that can be built in a few hours over a weekend. The bunk bed is particularly adaptable to a bedroom shared by two growing children.

WESTERN BUNK BEDS

If your children like the Old West and cowboys, they'll love sleeping in Western bunk beds. Parts are easy: four 2 × 6 × 5 feet; five 2 × 6 × 6 feet, 8 to 10 inches; and eight 2 × 6 × 3 feet, 5 inches.

First, make sure the wood is clean and sanded so that the children aren't hurt by splinters. Then, to make the head and foot of the bed, place the two 5-foot lengths 41 inches apart (or the width of the mattress you will use). Attach the 41-inch sections between the 5 footers, using wood screws. Place the screws about 5, 21, 37, and 53 inches from the top. The idea is to install them with approximately 12 inches between their edges. Do the same with the other two 5-foot sections and 41-inch boards.

Next, clamp the long 2-×-6 lumber and a 2-×-2-inch scrap of lumber of the same length together. Then drill five or six ½-inch holes about an inch from the bottom edge. Finally, run a bolt through the holes and attach the two pieces firmly together.

Attach these sides of the bed to the head and foot you previously made, using bolts, wood screws, or other fasteners. Install the rails about 10 or 12 inches off the floor.

Finally, cut and install slats to span the space between the rails and to support the box spring. Use metal brackets to attach the rails.

This plan can easily be modified to make it more decorative by using a jigsaw, router, or paint. But your youngsters might enjoy it most if it is left in the rough, just like a real bunk house.

SEMI-PRIVATE BUNK BED

Although the double decker bunk will not ensure the complete privacy many children want, some of the inconvenience of sharing a room can be alleviated by constructing bunks that provide a kind of semi-privacy.

On one side, build a plywood or wallboard partition up to the lower edge of the top bunk. On the opposite side, build the plywood wall from the lower edge of the top bunk upward to the ceiling. This produces, in effect, two separate sleeping compartments.

If the room is fairly large and of adequate proportions, this plan can be developed to make two separate rooms. From the wall opposite the end of the bunk, build a partition extending into the room. Allow sufficient space between the end of the bunk and the partition for passage. This partition should, of course, be built so that it is directly in line with the plywood board that closes off the side of the bottom bunk. It is sometimes practical to build a simple frame and hang a door at the end of the short partition so that the room is divided into two entirely separate sections.

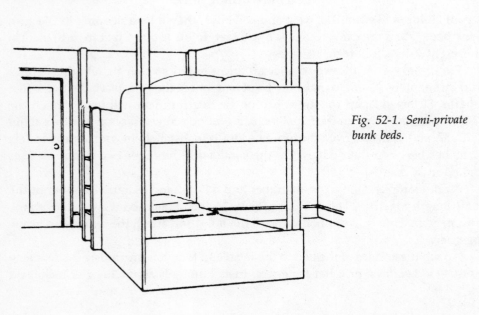

Fig. 52-1. Semi-private bunk beds.

The door will not guarantee complete privacy because the person in the inner room will still have to pass through the other part to the hall. Sometimes, however, the original room has two doors into the hall. When this is the case, a well-thought-out plan for placing the bunks will make it possible to divide the room in such a way that both small rooms have access to the hall. If the alteration is intended to be permanent, it might be worthwhile to cut a new doorway for the inner room. Keep in mind, though, that this complete division into two separate rooms is practical only when both sections can be provided with adequate light and ventilation.

The dividing partition may be made of plywood or of wallboard. Construct the partition on a frame of 2 × 4s attached to the floor and the wall. If it is a full-length wall, also attach it to the ceiling. Locate the partition so that it can be firmly nailed to the studs at the side and the joists overhead. Plaster can be removed at the point of contact with the wall to permit a firmer joint, but take care not to damage or loosen the plaster on either side of the new wall more than necessary. After the framework has been assembled on the floor, raise it into position, set with a plumb line, and nail in place. Cut wallboard pieces to fit over the frame and fasten so that the edges fit snugly against the lath where the partition joins the wall. Finish off the joints with plaster, and paper or paint the wall to match the rest of the room.

Index

Index